T0155595

# .NET Developer's Guide to Augmented Reality in iOS

## Building Immersive Apps Using Xamarin, ARKit, and C#

Lee Englestone

Apress®

*.NET Developer's Guide to Augmented Reality in iOS: Building Immersive Apps Using Xamarin, ARKit, and C#*

Lee Englestone
Offerton, UK

ISBN-13 (pbk): 978-1-4842-6769-1
https://doi.org/10.1007/978-1-4842-6770-7

ISBN-13 (electronic): 978-1-4842-6770-7

Managing Director, Apress Media LLC: Welmoed Spahr
Acquisitions Editor: Joan Murray
Development Editor: Laura Berendson
Coordinating Editor: Jill Balzano

Cover image designed by Freepik (www.freepik.com)

Distributed to the book trade worldwide by Springer Science+Business Media LLC, 1 New York Plaza, Suite 4600, New York, NY 10004. Phone 1-800-SPRINGER, fax (201) 348-4505, e-mail orders-ny@springer-sbm.com, or visit www.springeronline.com. Apress Media, LLC is a California LLC and the sole member (owner) is Springer Science + Business Media Finance Inc (SSBM Finance Inc). SSBM Finance Inc is a **Delaware** corporation.

For information on translations, please e-mail booktranslations@springernature.com; for reprint, paperback, or audio rights, please e-mail bookpermissions@springernature.com.

Apress titles may be purchased in bulk for academic, corporate, or promotional use. eBook versions and licenses are also available for most titles. For more information, reference our Print and eBook Bulk Sales web page at http://www.apress.com/bulk-sales.

Any source code or other supplementary material referenced by the author in this book is available to readers on GitHub via the book's product page, located at www.apress.com/9781484267691. For more detailed information, please visit http://www.apress.com/source-code.

Printed on acid-free paper

*This book is dedicated to my family.*

*To my amazing wife who is the kindest person you could ever hope to meet and my children, Holly and Aaron, who bring me so much joy.*

# Table of Contents

About the Author ................................................................................................ xi

About the Technical Reviewer ............................................................................ xiii

Preface ............................................................................................................... xv

Introduction ...................................................................................................... xvii

Chapter 1: Setting Up Your Environment .............................................................. 1

Apple ID.................................................................................................................. 1

Suitable iOS Device................................................................................................ 2

Install Xcode.......................................................................................................... 2

Install Visual Studio for Mac.................................................................................. 3

Create a New Project in Xcode............................................................................... 4

    Step 1. Choose a project template ..................................................................... 5

    Step 2. Provide project details........................................................................... 6

    Step 3. Provide a project location...................................................................... 7

    Step 4. View the new project............................................................................. 8

    Step 5. Select a Team or sign in with an Apple ID ............................................. 9

    Step 6. Change the deployment target............................................................. 10

    Step 7. Trust the developer.............................................................................. 11

    Step 8. Done .................................................................................................... 13

Create a New Project in Visual Studio for Mac..................................................... 13

    Step 1. Create a new project and select a project type..................................... 13

    Step 2. Provide app details.............................................................................. 14

    Step 3. Provide project details......................................................................... 15

    Step 4. Choose a deployment device and run .................................................. 16

    Set Camera Permissions ................................................................................. 17

Summary............................................................................................................... 18

## Chapter 2: Basic Concepts ...................................................................... 19

Scene View .............................................................................................. 19

Session .................................................................................................... 20

SceneKit .................................................................................................. 21

Positioning .............................................................................................. 21

World Origin ............................................................................................ 23

World Alignment ..................................................................................... 24

Gravity ..................................................................................................... 25

GravityAndHeading ................................................................................ 25

Camera ..................................................................................................... 25

Size .......................................................................................................... 26

Configuration .......................................................................................... 28

Summary .................................................................................................. 29

## Chapter 3: Nodes, Geometries, Materials, and Anchors ................... 31

Nodes ....................................................................................................... 31

Opacity ..................................................................................................... 32

Geometries .............................................................................................. 33

Built-in Geometry Shapes ...................................................................... 33

Materials .................................................................................................. 35

Solid Color Material ........................................................................... 35

Image Material ........................................................................................ 36

Material Fill Mode .................................................................................. 37

Anchors .................................................................................................... 38

Things to Try ........................................................................................... 38

Summary .................................................................................................. 39

## Chapter 4: Built-in AR Guides ............................................................. 41

Show Feature Points ............................................................................... 41

Show World Origin and Coordinate Axis .............................................. 42

Show Statistics ........................................................................................ 44

Coaching Overlay .................................................................................... 45

Summary.................................................................................................. 48

**Chapter 5: Animations** ........................................................................... **49**

Animating Opacity.................................................................................. 49

Animating Scale ..................................................................................... 50

Animating Position ................................................................................. 51

Animating Orientation ............................................................................ 51

Repeat Behavior..................................................................................... 52

Animation Easing ................................................................................... 53

Combining Animations ........................................................................... 54

Waiting ................................................................................................... 54

Summary.................................................................................................. 55

**Chapter 6: Constraints** ............................................................................ **57**

BillboardConstraint ................................................................................ 57

LookAtConstraint.................................................................................... 57

Other Constraints ................................................................................... 59

Things to Try........................................................................................... 59

Summary.................................................................................................. 59

**Chapter 7: Lighting** .................................................................................. **61**

Automatically Add Default Lighting......................................................... 61

Automatically Update Default Lighting.................................................... 61

Light Types ............................................................................................. 62

Adding Shadows ..................................................................................... 63

Things to Try........................................................................................... 67

Summary.................................................................................................. 68

**Chapter 8: Video and Sound** ................................................................... **69**

Playing Sound ........................................................................................ 69

Playing Video.......................................................................................... 70

Things to Try........................................................................................... 72

Summary.................................................................................................. 72

**Chapter 9: Plane Detection** ..................................................................... **73**

Detecting Planes ...................................................................................... 73

Remembering Planes ................................................................................ 73

ARSCNViewDelegate (Scene View Delegate) ......................................... 74

Plane Detection Example ......................................................................... 76

Turning Off Plane Detection ................................................................ 81

Possible Applications .......................................................................... 82

Things to Try ....................................................................................... 82

Summary .................................................................................................. 83

**Chapter 10: Image Detection** .................................................................. **85**

Adding Images as App Resources ........................................................... 85

Detecting the Images .......................................................................... 88

Dynamically Adding Images to Detect ................................................ 91

Things to Try ....................................................................................... 92

Summary .................................................................................................. 93

**Chapter 11: Face Tracking and Expression Detection** .......................... **95**

Tracking Faces ......................................................................................... 95

Recognize Facial Expressions ................................................................. 99

Things to Try ........................................................................................... 105

Summary ................................................................................................ 105

**Chapter 12: Touch Gestures and Interaction** ...................................... **107**

Gesture Recognizers .............................................................................. 107

Hooking Up Gesture Recognizers ........................................................... 108

Tapping ................................................................................................... 109

Pinching .................................................................................................. 110

Rotating .................................................................................................. 111

Panning ................................................................................................... 112

Swiping ................................................................................................... 113

Long Press ............................................................................................ 113

Things to Try....................................................................................... 114

Summary.............................................................................................. 115

**Chapter 13: 3D Models** ................................................................... **117**

Importing 3D Models........................................................................... 117

Creating Your Own 3D Models in Blender ......................................... 119

Add Shadows, Animations, and Make Interactive ............................. 121

Things to Try....................................................................................... 121

Summary.............................................................................................. 121

**Chapter 14: Physics** ......................................................................... **123**

Giving an Item a Rigid Structure ....................................................... 123

Applying Gravity to an Object............................................................ 124

Combining Gravity and Solid Objects ................................................ 125

Applying Force .................................................................................... 128

Things to Try....................................................................................... 132

Summary.............................................................................................. 133

**Chapter 15: Object Detection** .......................................................... **135**

Scanning and Saving Object Spatial Data.......................................... 135

Recognizing Scanned Objects............................................................. 137

Things to Try ................................................................................. 139

Summary.............................................................................................. 140

**Chapter 16: Body Tracking** .............................................................. **141**

Detecting a Body in a Scene .............................................................. 141

Capturing Body Motion....................................................................... 148

Potential Applications ......................................................................... 149

Things to Try....................................................................................... 150

Summary.............................................................................................. 150

**Chapter 17: Publishing to the App Store** ............................................................ **151**

App Store Submission To-Do List ................................................................................ 151

Set Up Icons for the App .............................................................................................. 152

Set Up Launch Screen Image ....................................................................................... 153

Set Up App ID and Entitlements ................................................................................... 154

Create and Install an App Store Provisioning Profile .................................................... 158

Update Build Release Configuration ............................................................................. 162

Set Up the App in App Store Connect ........................................................................... 164

Build the App and Submit It to Apple ........................................................................... 169

Summary ....................................................................................................................... 178

**Index** ....................................................................................................................... **179**

# About the Author

**Lee Englestone** is an innovative, hands-on software development manager and technical lead, based in Stockport, England. He has been a .NET developer for many years, writing code for Windows, web, mobile, cloud, and Augmented Reality (AR) applications in his spare time. He believes that there are many new exciting opportunities for developers in the area of Augmented Reality and is excited to share them with his fellow .NET developers. In recognition of his community contributions, he has been awarded a Microsoft MVP in Developer Technologies. He can be contacted through LinkedIn at `https://www.linkedin.com/in/leeenglestone/` or on Twitter at `https://twitter.com/LeeEnglestone`.

# About the Technical Reviewer

**Nishith Pathak** is India's first and only Artificial Intelligence (AI) Most Valuable Professional (MVP), a Microsoft Regional Director (RD), and a lead architect, speaker, AI thinker, innovator, and strategist. Nishith's expertise lies in helping Fortune 100 companies design and architect next-generation solutions that incorporate AI, ML, cognitive services, Blockchain, and many more. He also laid his expertise in defining and strategizing technology road maps for customers and companies using emerging technologies. He sits on several technical advisory boards across the globe. He has also authored more than half a dozen international books for Springer Publication, United States. The last three books were on Artificial Intelligence (AI). Earlier, Nishith has also played the role of a PAN account enterprise architect where he was responsible for the overall architecture to design in multiple projects. He is an internationally acclaimed speaker on technologies like AI, IOT, and Blockchain and regularly speaks at various technical conferences. He advices and mentors a lot of startups as a community initiative.

For his expertise on Artificial Intelligence, Microsoft have awarded him the first Most Valuable Professional (MVP) from India in the Artificial Intelligence category. He is the only Artificial Intelligence MVP in India to date. Globally, he is among 19 MVPs on AI, recognized by Microsoft for their sheer expertise on AI. He has also received the "Microsoft Regional Director" award which is awarded to 150 of the world's top technology visionaries chosen specifically for their proven cross-platform expertise.

Nishith is a gold member and sits on the advisory board of various national and international computer science societies and organizations. Nishith is currently working as Global Chief Technologist for Emerging Technologies and Advanced Analytics for DXC Technology where he is focused on using emerging technologies helping companies architect solutions based on these technologies, laying out technology road maps, and curating the startup ecosystem. He can be contacted at nispathak@gmail.com or through LinkedIn at www.linkedin.com/in/nishithpathak/.

# Preface

I have always loved futuristic science fiction films and TV series. As a child, I remember fondly watching *Star Trek* and *Star Wars* with my dad most evenings after school. You name it, if it was set in the future, I probably watched it.

But these days, it is not the lasers or spaceships that I marvel at. Being a software developer, it is the glowing, floating futuristic-looking computer interfaces that spark my imagination. It seems in some distant future we are destined to shed our monitors, mice, and keyboards and replace them with floating transparent holograms using only our hands to interact with them.

Having followed Augmented Reality very closely for some time, I believe that future is already here, and to prove it, I will show you how to build the interfaces of tomorrow, today. As .NET developers, we have the enviable ability to develop apps for a wide range of uses including Windows, web, console, cloud, serverless, ML, AI, mobile, and now Augmented Reality.

I'm very excited to share how you and fellow .NET developers can use .NET and C# to create amazing apps that use Augmented Reality to open up a new world of possibilities, to be at the forefront of unique AR experiences that will take the world by storm.

# Introduction

Welcome to the start of your journey into the exciting world of Augmented Reality development.

Being a .NET developer and iPhone user for many years, I was shocked when I accidentally stumbled onto the Augmented Reality functionality that .NET developers can target and leverage to create fantastic user experiences; I was amazed that more .NET developers weren't using the techniques outlined in this book to create their own AR apps for their own iOS devices, especially at a time when Augmented Reality is becoming increasingly popular in our society and adopted by a growing number of industries and markets.

In fact, I was so impressed by the possibilities that Augmented Reality offers .NET developers that I started experimenting with it as much as possible, as well as discussing it at .NET user groups around the country to show fellow .NET developers the kind of experiences they could achieve.

But I didn't stop there, I wondered how else I could reach even more .NET developers to share with them this new way of creating immersive user experiences. I even wondered if I could write a book introducing the concept of .NET: this book. And if you are reading this, you are interested in learning how to create the next generation of Augmented Reality user experiences and have come to the right place.

Before we get stuck into coding and creating, it is worth giving you an overview of Augmented Reality and how to use this book.

## What Is Augmented Reality?

Augmented Reality (or AR for short) is the process of a computer program or mobile app making something appear in your immediate (real-world) environment that isn't actually there. That object's position is maintained in the real world and as you move around and change your perspective.

INTRODUCTION

All of the major technology companies are finding uses for Augmented Reality including Facebook, Apple, Google, and Microsoft. At the time of writing, if you Google "tiger" on a mobile device, you are presented with a screen where if you press "View in 3D," you can view the animal in Augmented Reality as shown in the image on the right in Figure 1.

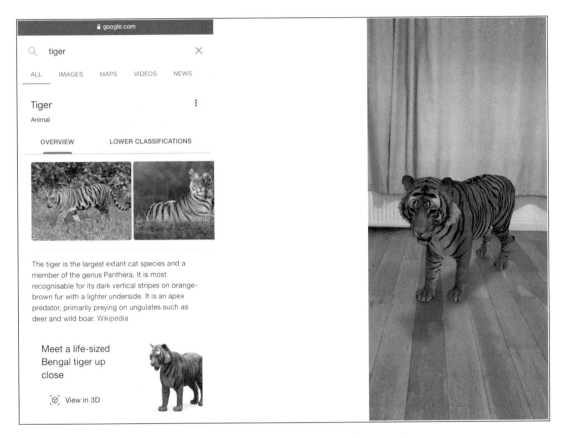

***Figure 1.*** *Augmented reality is becoming increasingly popular*

Augmented Reality isn't to be confused with Virtual Reality (or VR for short), where you wear a headset that completely occludes your vision and everything you see is a product of the running computer program or mobile app.

One of the most popular VR devices on the market is Facebook's Oculus range of devices with perhaps their most popular VR game being *Beat Saber* where one must use slice cubes that are approaching the player in VR to the rhythm of the music.

For completion, you may also have heard the terms XR (Extended Reality) and MR (Mixed Reality) previously. These terms are generally referring to *both* Augmented and Virtual Reality. We won't use or discuss the terms XR and MR further in this book; you may just be interested to know that those terms encompass both AR and VR.

# Who Is This Book For?

This book is for .NET developers that want to use C# and Xamarin to create Augmented Reality apps for their iOS devices. While experience with Xamarin cross-platform apps and Visual Studio for Mac is helpful, it is not necessary, as we will cover the environment setup and basic concepts early on.

You may already be familiar with Augmented Reality, you may just be curious to learn more about what is possible with it, or you may already have an idea for an Augmented Reality app that you wish to create.

The only thing you need is your imagination.

# How to Read This Book

This book has been written to introduce you to the fundamental building blocks and concepts used to create Augmented Reality experiences, then show how these can be combined together, then move on to explain more advanced concepts. At each stage, code samples are provided to allow you to experiment for yourself the concept being described.

While I encourage you to understand each topic before moving on to the next, rest assured most code samples are stand-alone and can be run without previous code samples. So if you want to try out image detection before fully understanding how to work with simple geometries, feel free to do so.

# Code Samples

Code samples in this book have been written with clarity in mind. I'm sure in most cases the code could be optimized or better structured. They have been written to aid understanding and may not be the same code I would necessarily recommend be used for production.

Code samples can also be found in the source code for the companion app on GitHub.

# Companion App

All of the example functionality described in this book including face detection, 3D models, and so on can be experienced using the free companion app available in the iOS App Store as shown in Figure 2. The code for the companion app itself is in GitHub so that you can clone it to your computer and play around with the code yourself.

***Figure 2.*** *Example ARKit functionality is shown in the companion app*

# The Rise of Augmented Reality

The rise of Augmented Reality has been a slow but steady one. That's not necessarily a bad thing given how Virtual Reality has suffered from being overhyped for over a decade and only recently delivering what it originally promised.

The slow adoption of Augmented Reality on the other hand has been relative to the increasing sophistication of our mobile devices, especially their processors and cameras. It is not uncommon for some mobile phones to boast three or four different cameras, some of which can determine the depth of field of what they are being directed at. Those cameras along with increasingly powerful processors are continually helping make Augmented Reality environments more accurate and allowing increasingly advanced experiences.

It isn't surprising then that a number of Augmented Reality frameworks allowing developers to leverage these devices have sprung up, the most common being ARCore for Android and ARKit for iOS.

You need only look at the popularity of one of the very first Augmented Reality games, *Pokémon Go*, that launched in 2016 which made over 30 billion (yes, billion) dollars for evidence that the general public are not only willing to embrace Augmented Reality but they desire to and are willing to pay to do so.

# ARKit

In 2017, Apple introduced its Augmented Reality framework ARKit to the world and has been improving it every year since. ARKit makes use of your device's camera, gyroscope, and accelerometer to determine the direction your device is pointing and the differences between camera frames so it can maintain the Augmented Reality experience.

## ARKit 1.0 (September 2017)

ARKit was first introduced in iOS 11.0 with the ability to track the world and environment around the user. This initial release also allowed for face tracking and horizontal plane detection.

## ARKit 1.5 (March 2018)

In their first ARKit update in iOS 11.3, Apple added the much requested ability to detect vertical planes such as walls as well as simple image recognition.

# ARKit 2.0 (September 2018)

Later that year in iOS 12 ARKit was extended to allow 3D object recognition as well as scene persistence and sharing.

# ARKit 3.0 (September 2019)

In iOS 13 Apple added support for people occlusion, multiple face tracking, as well as human body tracking.

# ARKit 3.5 (March 2020)

In iOS 13.4 Apple added LiDAR scanning to iPad Pro devices improving plane detection as well as introducing Scene Geometry allowing users to create topological maps of their surroundings and even use semantic classification which can identify everyday objects such as chairs and tables. Though this is just for iPad Pro at the time of writing, it may be supported by future versions of iPhone and is rumored to be in iPhone 12.

# Augmented Reality for .NET Developers Using Xamarin

Until fairly recently, if you wanted to create a native Augmented Reality app for iOS using ARKit, you would have to write it in Objective-C or Swift using Xcode.

Note: This book covers Augmented Reality development using Xamarin and ARKit which is Apple's Augmented Reality framework. This is not to be confused with ARCore which is Android's Augmented Reality framework.

A company called Xamarin (founded in 2011), seeing how people wanted to develop mobile apps for different platforms, created a framework called Mono which allowed C# developers to write C# code and produce apps able to run on macOS, Linux, Android, and iOS.

So popular was Xamarin in fact that in February 2016 Microsoft came along and acquired them and ported ARKit (among other frameworks) to .NET. Soon after that Microsoft made it possible for .NET developers to use Visual Studio for Mac, Xamarin, and ARKit to create Augmented Reality applications and deploy them to iOS devices.

Interestingly while this is a fantastic way to allow .NET developers to create Augmented Reality iOS apps using C#, there aren't many people doing it just yet. On the upside, you can be one of the first .NET developers to create and share some amazing AR experiences; on the downside, most of the ARKit code samples you will find online will be in Objective-C or Swift, and it can take a slight bit of head-scratching to work out how to do the same thing in .NET.

This is where this book comes in (I have spent many an hour translating Swift ARKit examples to C# so you don't have to). You're welcome.

# The Future of Augmented Reality

We are on the verge of an Augmented Reality revolution. While we are currently addicted to our little black screens to get our daily dose of news, social interaction, and entertainment, they will soon be replaced by Augmented Reality experiences.

Admittedly these Augmented Reality experiences are currently predominantly on our mobile devices; however, there are an ever-increasing number of manufacturers producing Augmented Reality headsets that will soon flood the market. It is therefore only logical that there will be a large demand of Augmented Reality software development and experiences needed to operate on these headsets.

Once businesses, marketers, and entrepreneurs start to realize the potential and leverage the power of Augmented Reality, we will see a gold rush of Augmented Reality experiences. Believe me, you want to be on the ground floor, build your AR skills, and ride the rocket that will be Augmented Reality development.

# Summary

We discussed Augmented Reality and how you can use your existing knowledge of C# and .NET along with the ARKit framework to create your own Augmented Reality experiences. We discussed just how exciting the future of Augmented Reality is going to be, especially for us .NET developers who get to create experiences for them.

So now that you can't wait to start producing Augmented Reality experiences, you'll want to check out the next chapter, "Setting Up Your Environment," which will tell you exactly what you need to do to get started as quickly as possible.

# CHAPTER 1

# Setting Up Your Environment

First, we need to start by making sure you have a few things installed that you will need; after that, we can begin writing and deploying basic Augmented Reality apps to your iOS device.

Here is a list of the things you are going to need:

- An Apple ID

- A suitable iOS device

- A computer running macOS

- Xcode

- Visual Studio for Mac

## Apple ID

Good news, you do not need to enroll in the paid Apple Developer Program to deploy apps to your iOS devices; you just need your Apple ID to get started. However, should you wish to eventually publish an app to the App Store, you will need to join and pay for the Apple Developer Program. You can find more information about the Apple Developer Program at `https://developer.apple.com/programs/`.

© Lee Englestone 2021
L. Englestone, *.NET Developer's Guide to Augmented Reality in iOS*,
https://doi.org/10.1007/978-1-4842-6770-7_1

# Suitable iOS Device

While ARKit has been around since iOS 11, older phones may not have sophisticated enough cameras or CPUs to use some of the newer features of ARKit such as body occlusion at all. You will need at least an iPhone 6s or newer iPhone to use Augmented Reality examples in this book.

It's also worth mentioning that you will need the appropriate cable to connect your device to your PC or laptop so that you can deploy the app from Xcode and Visual Studio for Mac to it. It is worth noting that after a little setup it is also possible to deploy your app to your device from your computer over Wi-Fi without the need for a cable.

# Install Xcode

While we will predominantly be using Visual Studio for Mac to create the Augmented Reality apps throughout this book, Xcode is required among other reasons to provision and install code signing certificates for our app onto your iOS device.

If you don't already have Xcode installed, you can install it from the App Store (Figure 1-1).

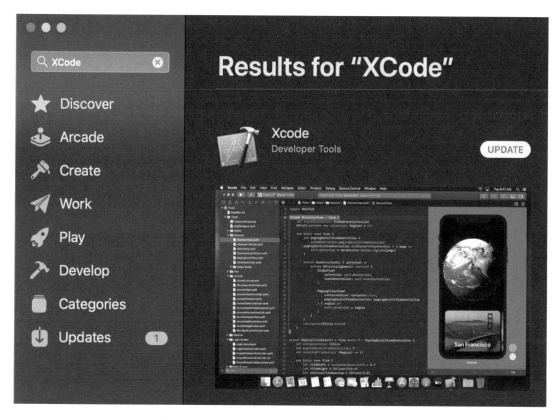

***Figure 1-1.*** *Download and install Xcode from the App Store*

# Install Visual Studio for Mac

You will also need the latest version of Visual Studio for Mac, which at the time of writing is 2019, and you'll be glad to hear we will be spending most of our time in it. I have found that as Visual Studio for Mac is a fairly new product, it is constantly being updated with improvements.

If you are a user of Visual Studio on Windows, you will notice that while Visual Studio for Mac is similar to Visual Studio for Windows, it does have some differences; they are not 100% equivalent.

There are a number of requirements for Visual Studio for Mac, the main one being Xcode (`https://docs.microsoft.com/en-us/visualstudio/productinfo/vs2019-system-requirements-mac`).

You can install Visual Studio for Mac from `https://visualstudio.microsoft.com/vs/mac/` as can be seen in Figure 1-2.

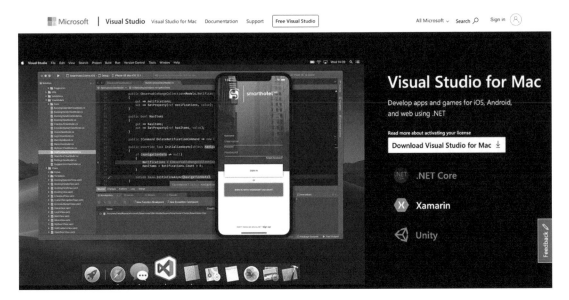

***Figure 1-2.*** *Download and install Visual Studio for Mac*

# Create a New Project in Xcode

Once you have Xcode and Visual Studio for Mac installed, let's start creating our very first project. If you are wondering why we are starting with a project in Xcode, it is because we need to create a blank app in Xcode and deploy it to our device, in order to deploy the relevant code signing certificates to the device.

Launch Xcode and choose "Create a new Xcode project" as shown in Figure 1-3.

*Figure 1-3.* *Create a new project in Xcode*

## Step 1. Choose a project template

On the next screen titled "Choose a template for your new project:" when you come to choose a template, choose "Single View App" and then click "Next" as shown in Figure 1-4.

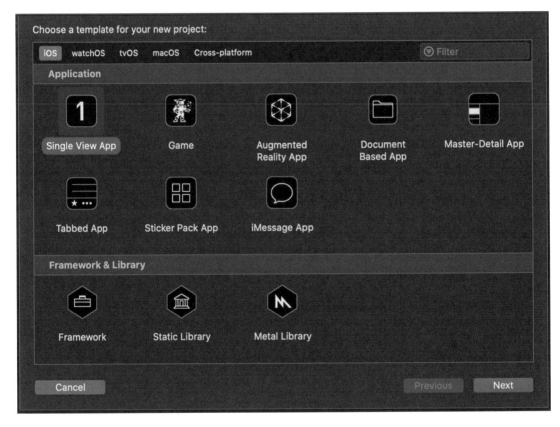

***Figure 1-4.*** *Choose "Single View App" as the project template*

## Step 2. Provide project details

On the next screen titled "Choose options for your new project:" provide a name for your app in the "Product Name" field. In Figure 1-5, you can see I have made up some details.

If you have signed into Xcode before using your Apple ID, you may already have a (Personal Team) entry in the Team field. If not, don't worry. We will sign in to generate a Team later.

You can leave Language and User Interface as the default; also, we won't be using Unit Tests or UI Tests so you might as well untick them.

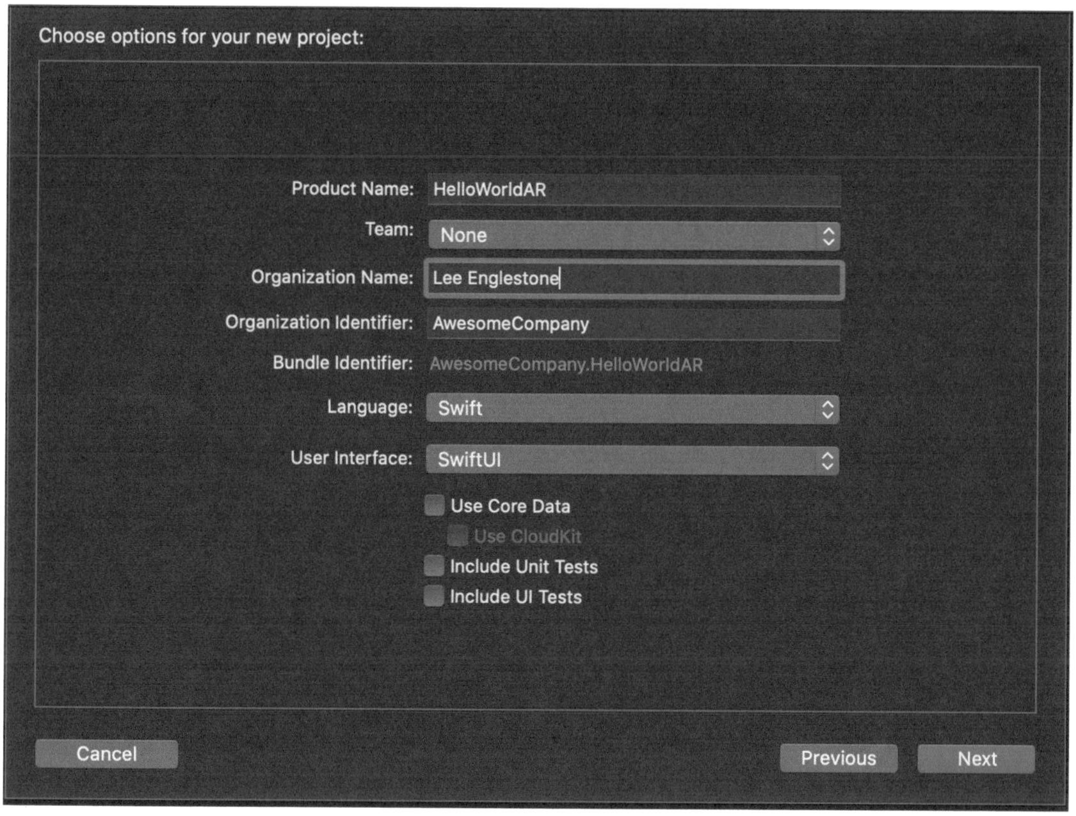

Choose options for your new project:

| | |
|---|---|
| Product Name: | HelloWorldAR |
| Team: | None |
| Organization Name: | Lee Englestone |
| Organization Identifier: | AwesomeCompany |
| Bundle Identifier: | AwesomeCompany.HelloWorldAR |
| Language: | Swift |
| User Interface: | SwiftUI |

☐ Use Core Data
☐ Use CloudKit
☐ Include Unit Tests
☐ Include UI Tests

Cancel                                              Previous        Next

***Figure 1-5.*** *Provide project option details*

**Note**    Pay particular attention to the Bundle Identifier that is created as we will need this when we create our Augmented Reality app in Visual Studio for Mac.

In this example, it is AwesomeCompany.HelloWorldAR.

Click Next.

# Step 3. Provide a project location

Choose a location for your project. I generally create a new folder for this.

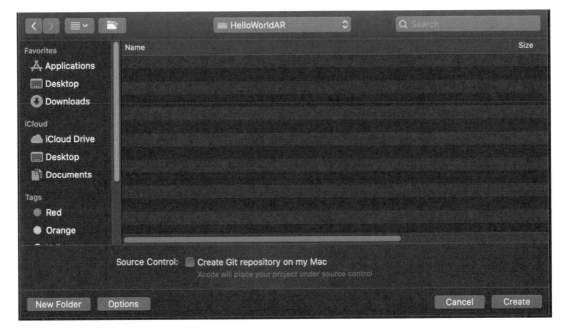

***Figure 1-6.*** *Choose a location for your project*

Click Create.

# Step 4. View the new project

You should see the newly created Swift project in Xcode as in Figure 1-7. Don't worry about this too much. We won't be changing any of this Swift code!

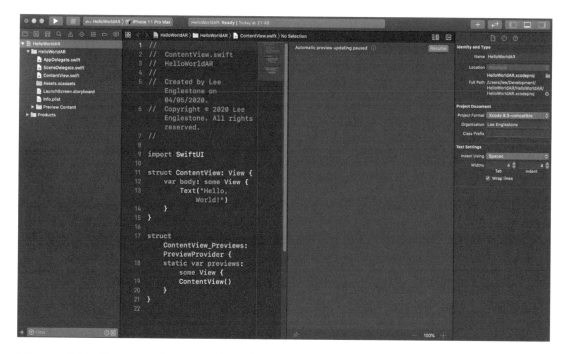

***Figure 1-7.*** *Your newly created Swift project*

We will however be deploying that project to our device to generate and deploy the required code signing certificates that we need later.

You'll be glad to hear this is the final step in the hoop jumping required before we can concentrate on working in Visual Studio for Mac with C# code.

If you click the Play button or run the project now and didn't provide a Team earlier, the build will fail. So let's go and choose a Team.

# Step 5. Select a Team or sign in with an Apple ID

Double-click the project name to open the project settings, and then go to the Signing & Capabilities section.

If a Team isn't already in the list, select "Add an Account..." from the list and sign in with your Apple ID as shown in Figure 1-8.

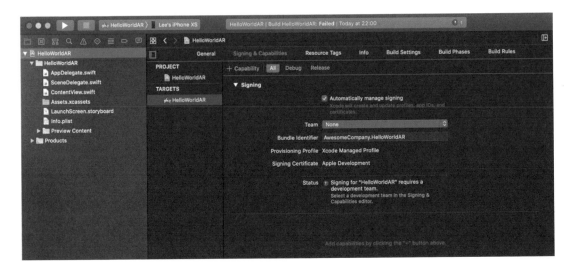

**Figure 1-8.** *Choose a development Team*

# Step 6. Change the deployment target

If you run the project now, it will launch the Device Simulator. We don't want that, so make sure your computer is connected to your device via an appropriate cable, and then change the deployment target to your device name (as shown in Figure 1-9) and click play or run (making sure your device is unlocked).

---

**Note**    It is possible to set up debugging and deployment over Wi-Fi, removing the need for a cable between your computer and device.

---

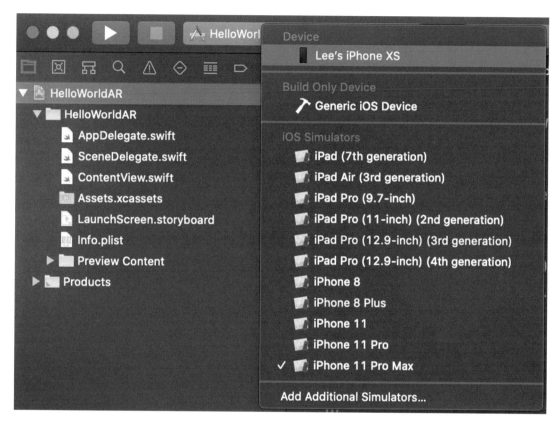

**Figure 1-9.** *Change deployment target*

# Step 7. Trust the developer

If you run the project now, it will deploy the app to the device; however, you may see the following message shown in Figure 1-10 if you have not deployed to your device previously. Don't worry. This just means that there is a simple security step we need to do on your device.

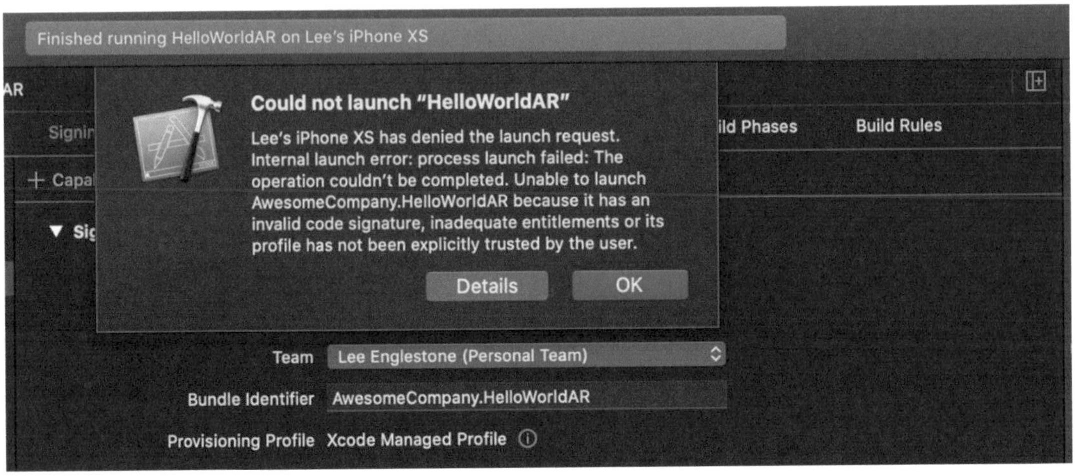

Finished running HelloWorldAR on Lee's iPhone XS

**Could not launch "HelloWorldAR"**

Lee's iPhone XS has denied the launch request.
Internal launch error: process launch failed: The
operation couldn't be completed. Unable to launch
AwesomeCompany.HelloWorldAR because it has an
invalid code signature, inadequate entitlements or its
profile has not been explicitly trusted by the user.

Details          OK

Team          Lee Englestone (Personal Team)

Bundle Identifier  AwesomeCompany.HelloWorldAR

Provisioning Profile  Xcode Managed Profile ⓘ

***Figure 1-10.*** *Trust developer*

In order to trust the developer and your app on your iOS device, you have to go to
Settings ➤ General ➤ Device Management and select the Developer App.

And press the Trust button and confirm as shown in Figure 1-11.

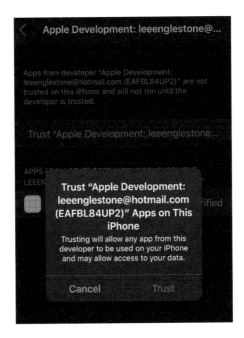

***Figure 1-11.*** *Trust developer in device management*

If you run the app now from Xcode and all has gone to plan, you should see the default Hello world screen on your phone.

## Step 8. Done

Congratulations. For some this may be the first time you have ever deployed an application to your device. And you'll be pleased to know we won't be doing anything else with this project. However, you may need this project to redeploy certificates to your device so I wouldn't delete it. Just keep it around on your machine.

---

**Note**    Personal code signing only lasts for 7 days, after which you will need to redeploy your app to your device to make it work again.

---

**Reminder**    Make sure you make a note of the Bundle Identifier in step 2 as we will need this when we create our app in Visual Studio for Mac.

---

# Create a New Project in Visual Studio for Mac

Next, we are going to create our app which will contain our Augmented Reality experiments in Visual Studio for Mac and deploy it to our iOS device.

Launch Visual Studio for Mac and choose New Project.

## Step 1. Create a new project and select a project type

From the list of template categories, select iOS, and then select Single View App as shown in Figure 1-12.

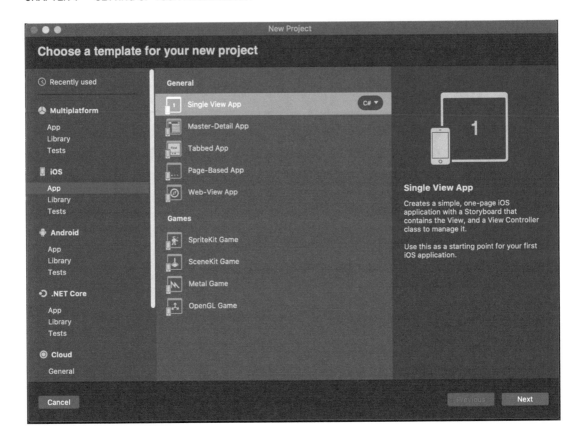

*Figure 1-12.*  *Choose a project type*

## Step 2. Provide app details

You will want to use the same App Name and Organization Identifier that you used in your Xcode app so that the Bundle Identifier is *Identical* to the Xcode one as shown in Figure 1-13. This is so that the same code signing certificates can be used to provision and deploy the app to your iOS device.

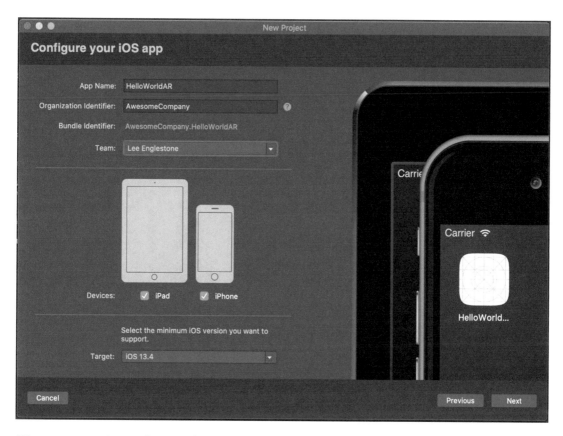

***Figure 1-13.*** *Provide app details*

## Step 3. Provide project details

Now you need to provide the project name, solution name, and location for your project as shown in Figure 1-14. These can be whatever you want, but make sure you provide a different location to the Xcode app.

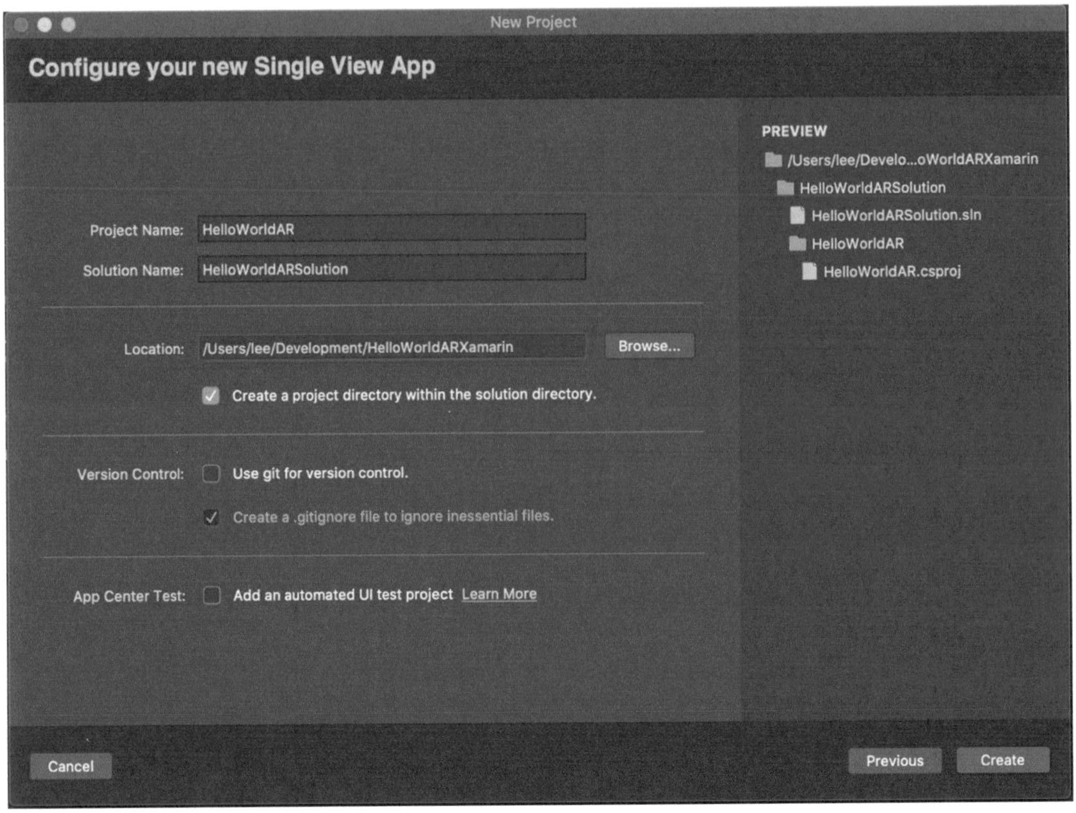

**Figure 1-14.** *Provide project details*

Click Create.

# Step 4. Choose a deployment device and run

After creating your project in the previous step, you should see the newly created project skeleton as in Figure 1-15.

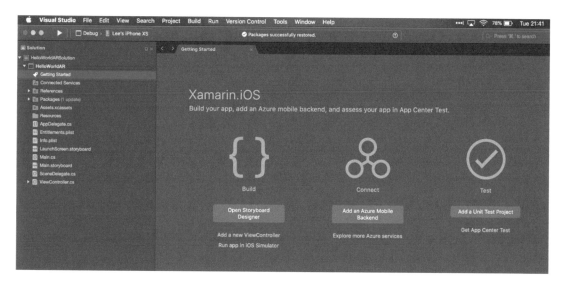

**Figure 1-15.**  *View the new project*

Make sure you change the deployment destination to the connected iOS device and that the device is unlocked, then run the project. The device should run the app which is a rather boring blank white screen.

Congratulations! You have deployed your first .NET iOS project to your device.

It's worth noting that there is nothing Augmented Reality about this app yet; we haven't written the code for this yet. The project that you have created and the app that you have deployed will host all of the Augmented Reality functionality that we will cover in this book.

# Set Camera Permissions

Your new app that we will use for Augmented Reality will need to use your camera, so you will need to explicitly declare this permission in the projects Info.plist file.

You do this by choosing "Privacy – Camera Usage Description" from the drop-down list and providing any message you like as shown in Figure 1-16. This message will be shown the first time the app is ran to ask the user to grant the app permissions to use the camera.

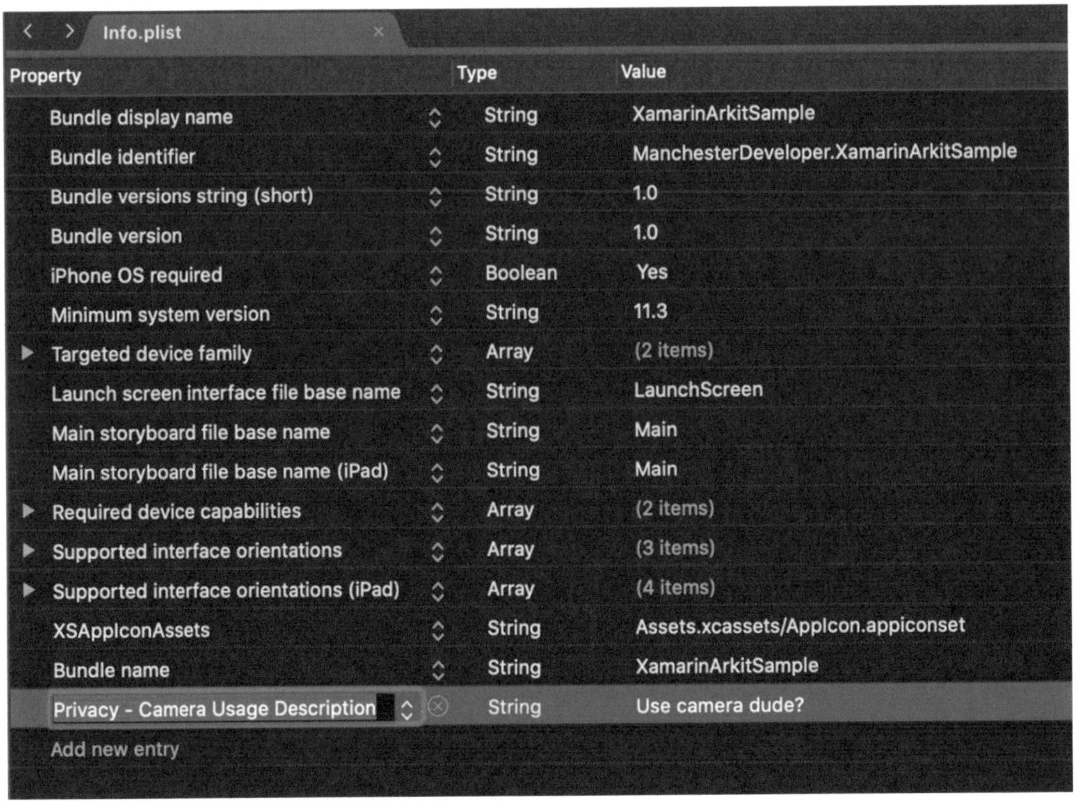

*Figure 1-16.*  *Set camera permissions*

# Summary

You should now have your local environment all set up and ready to start experimenting with Augmented Reality. And that is exactly what we will do, but first let's discuss some of the basic concepts of Augmented Reality and ARKit in the next chapter.

# CHAPTER 2

# Basic Concepts

In this chapter, we look at a few basic concepts that make mobile Augmented Reality experiences using ARKit possible and that you will use to build your Augmented Reality apps very soon.

It is important to gain a good understanding of the basics before continuing as this will put you in good stead before moving on to further topics in the book where we will refer back to some of these basics. Only after gaining an appreciation of these basic concepts will we move on to exploring more advanced concepts.

## Scene View

In ARKit, the Augmented Reality SceneView (`ARSCNView`) is where all the magic happens. When the session of an `ARSCNView` runs, it sets the camera to be the background of the View and shows anything we have added to the scene overlaid on top.

In Listing 2-1, you can see that the Scene View is created in the ViewController constructor and that it is possible to set some initial properties (that we will discuss later). This SceneView is then added as a subview of the current view.

In the `ViewDidLoad` event, we are also setting the SceneView's Frame to be this view's Frame.

You will be using this basic *setup/boilerplate* code in all of the AR examples throughout the book.

***Listing 2-1.*** Creating the Scene View

```
private readonly ARSCNView sceneView;

public ViewController(IntPtr handle) : base(handle)
{
    this.sceneView = new ARSCNView();
```

© Lee Englestone 2021
L. Englestone, .NET Developer's Guide to Augmented Reality in iOS,
https://doi.org/10.1007/978-1-4842-6770-7_2

```
    {
        AutoenablesDefaultLighting = true
    };

    this.View.AddSubview(this.sceneView);
}

public override void ViewDidLoad()
{
    base.ViewDidLoad();
    this.sceneView.Frame = this.View.Frame;
}
```

# Session

Nothing happens in your SceneView until you call the `Session.Run()` method. Once the session starts running, it does a number of things.

First, it sets the camera as the background for the view.

Then as you move your device/camera around, it starts trying to understand your immediate environment, noting points of interest and their relative positions between camera frames while using the device's gyroscope and accelerometer to understand the orientation of the device. The fancy name for this is Visual Inertial Odometry, and this is how it is able to understand the environment and persist the location of things we put into the scene when we move the camera around.

It starts placing invisible `Anchors` at points of interest it finds as well as overlaying any 3D objects you have placed into the scene at the locations you placed them. Anchors (which we will discuss more of in Chapter 3, "Nodes, Geometries, Materials, and Anchors") are points of reference in our AR scene that are either automatically detected or manually placed in the scene.

When calling the `Session.Run()` method, you must provide a type of `ARConfiguration` which defines the type of AR functionality you want to use in the scene as shown in Listing 2-2. Depending on the configuration type and settings used in the session, it may behave differently depending on what it has detected in the scenes, such as planes, images, or faces.

***Listing 2-2.*** Starting the SceneView Session

```
public override void ViewDidAppear(bool animated)
{
    base.ViewDidAppear(animated);

    this.sceneView.Session.Run(
        new ARWorldTrackingConfiguration());
}
```

# SceneKit

While ARKit makes possible the Augmented Reality capabilities mentioned in this book, we will actually be using SceneKit (which is Apple's 3D graphics framework) extensively including to place objects into our AR scenes. The following sections "Size" and "Positioning" are all from SceneKit as are Nodes, Geometries, and Materials which will be discussed in the next chapter and Animations that we will be discussing in Chapter 5, "Animations."

If you are wondering where ARKit ends and SceneKit begins, the following may help.

You can usually tell which code types come from ARKit or SceneKit as they are generally prefixed with AR or SCN, respectively. For example, `ARSCNView` is from ARKit and `SCNNode` is from SceneKit.

# Positioning

It is important to know how the coordinates system works in SceneKit so that you can orientate yourself around an AR scene, as well as being able to place multiple objects around your environment in three-dimensional space.

There are three dimensions you need to remember and get used to, X, Y, and Z illustrated by Figure 2-1. Where X is left to right, Y is down to up and Z is front to back. Fortunately, there is a built-in feature you can turn on that shows the coordinate axis actually within your app. We will cover this in Chapter 4, "Built-in AR Guides."

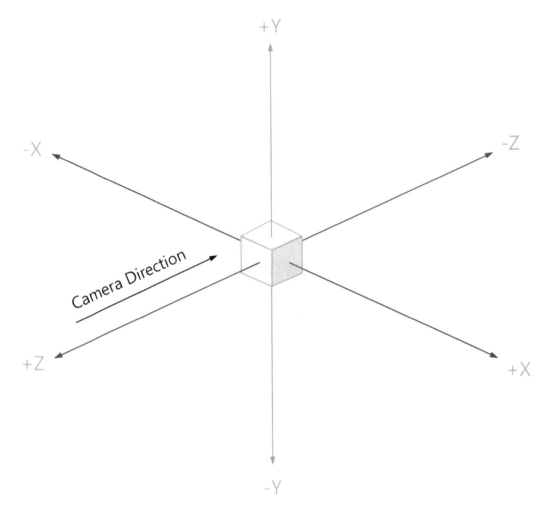

**Figure 2-1.** *Coordinates system*

In Listing 2-3, we can see that when setting the position of an object, we use an instance of SCNVector3 and provide values for the X, Y, and Z coordinates which are floating point values where 1f is effectively 1 meter, 0.1f 10 centimeters, and 0.01f 1 centimeter.

Once we have created an instance of SCNVector3, effectively declaring a position in 3D space, we can set a nodes position to it using a nodes Position property.

*Listing 2-3.* Setting the position of an object in 3D space

```
public override void ViewDidAppear(bool animated)
{
    base.ViewDidAppear(animated);

    this.sceneView.Session.Run(new
      ARWorldTrackingConfiguration());

    // Creates and assigns a position to a node
    // In this case it is setting it 1m above and 1m in front
    // of the devices initial position
    var position = new SCNVector3(0, 1f, -1f);
    var node = new SCNNode();
    node.Position = position;

    // Adds the node to the scene
    // (will be invisible as we haven't told it what
    // to look like yet)
    this.sceneView.Scene.RootNode.AddChildNode(node);
}
```

It is probably worth noting that you can always change an object's position after you have placed it in the scene by simply updating its Position property with an instance of SCNVector3 with different X, Y, and Z coordinate values.

---

**Hint**    It took me a while to remember that to place an object in front of me, I had to place it with a negative Z value (which is in front of you). Placing an item in the positive Z axis actually places it behind you. Doh! Many a time I have been left confused looking for an object I placed in the scene in front of me, when actually it was behind me!

---

# World Origin

By default, when you start your AR app, your world origin is the point that your device was located when the app is started. This position of your default world origin will be (0,0,0) where X, Y, and Z are all 0. Regardless of where you physically move your device in relation to the world origin, all objects you place in your scene will be relative to that world origin, *not* the current position of your device. That said, it is possible to programmatically change the position of the world origin after your app has started if you need to.

So accurate is the position of the world origin in the AR experiences you create, that you will even notice different perspectives depending on whether you are sitting down or standing when you launch your app.

It is worth noting that if you don't explicitly set the position of an object when you add it to a scene, it will be placed at this world origin (0,0,0).

---

**Hint**    If you place a fairly large object at the world origin, you may not see it because unless you have changed your physical position, you are effectively occupying the same space as (or are inside) the virtual object. In this scenario, you may have to physically take a step back to see something that is placed at the world origin, as it will then be in front of you. Or alternatively when placing something in the scene, give it a -Z value to place it in front of you.

---

As you can imagine, the world origin is important because it becomes almost a tether or central reference point for your scene or AR experience.

# World Alignment

When your ARSession starts, its ARWorldTrackingConfiguration will use a particular WorldAlignment value to determine by default the setup and behavior of the axis within your app as well as its initial orientation.

It is important because it will determine which way is forward (-Z) and therefore which way is left (-X) and right (+X), as well as which way is up (Y) and therefore which way is down (-Y).

If we desire, we are able to change the default WorldAlignment property of the ARWorldTrackingConfiguration which is WorldAlignment.Gravity.

As well as Gravity, there are three different WorldAlignment settings you can use which make your axis work in different ways.

# Gravity

The Y axis is parallel to gravity, that is, straight down; the other axes are aligned to the initial orientation of the device when the app is started. That is, -Z is the direction the device was facing when the app was launched, -X to the left, X the right, and +Z behind.

For example, using this option and placing an object into the scene with the coordinates (0, 0, -1f) will place it 1 m from the world origin in the direction the app was facing when it started. If you closed the app, turned the direction you were facing, then launched the app again, and again placed an object into the scene at (0, 0, -1f), it will appear 1 m from the world origin in the direction you are now facing.

In most cases, `WorldAlignment = ARWorldAlignment.Gravity` will give your axis the behavior you desire, so I'd recommend you stick with using this for the time being.

# GravityAndHeading

Again, the Y axis is parallel to gravity, though this time the Z axis is aligned to North and South and the X axis to East and West. That is, -Z is always the direction of North, +Z South, -X West, and +X East.

I imagine you may want to use this setting if you are building some sort of navigation functionality. Using this setting effectively turns your axis into a compass which will always make your axis orientated to North, South, East, and West.

For example, using this option and placing an object into the scene with the coordinates (0, 0, -1f) will place it 1 m from the world origin in the direction of magnetic North, and therefore placing something at (-1f, 0, 0) will place it 1 m West of your current location, and so forth.

For both `Gravity` and `GravityAndHeading`, any position along the Y axis is aligned with gravity with -Y going straight down toward the center of the earth and +Y straight up away from the center of the earth.

# Camera

This setting works very differently to both `Gravity` and `GravityHeading`. Using `WorldAlignment.Camera` sets the coordinates system of the scene to match the orientation of the camera at all times, therefore making -Z always aligned to the direction you are facing, -X always to your left, and Y upward from the camera. How you orientate the camera will have an effect on the axis system, including which direction the Y axis is aligned to.

If these World Alignments seem confusing right now, do not worry too much. One great way of getting used to them is by turning on a debug flag which places a visual representation of the X, Y, and Z axes into the scene at the world origin, something that is very useful when experimenting with your first AR experiences. We will look at how to do this in Chapter 4, "Built-in AR Guides."

# Size

Sizes in ARKit (well, actually SceneKit remember?) are stored as float data types where a value of 1f is equivalent to 1 meter, which means 0.1f is the equivalent of 10 centimeters and 0.01f is 1 centimeter. It is useful to bear this in mind as it is easy to make something too big (and you cannot see it because you are inside it!) or too far away. Coincidentally animating the size and position of something in AR scenes can produce a nice effect, something we will learn how to do in Chapter 5, "Animations."

In Figure 2-2, we can see the relative sizes of boxes that are 1 cm, 10 cm, 50 m, and 1 m, respectively, and the code that created them in Listings 2-4 and 2-5.

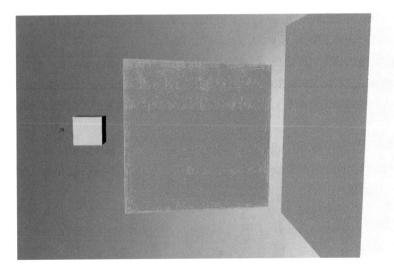

***Figure 2-2.*** *Virtual objects with different sizes*

This time  as shown in Listing 2-4 in the ViewDidAppear method (where we will implement most of our AR code throughout this book), we are creating four different instances of CubeNode (a custom class that we have inherited from SCNNode that can be seen in Listing 2-5) of varying sizes and adding them to the scene using the important method called `this.sceneView.Scene.RootNode.AddChildNode()`.

We will look at SCNNodes in more detail in the next chapter, "Nodes, Geometries, Materials, and Anchors."

***Listing 2-4.***  Adding objects of different sizes

```
public override void ViewDidAppear(bool animated)
{
    base.ViewDidAppear(animated);

    this.sceneView.Session.Run(
      new ARWorldTrackingConfiguration());

    // 1cm
    var cubeNode1 = new CubeNode(0.01f, UIColor.Red);
    cubeNode1.Position = new SCNVector3(0, 0, 0);

    // 10cm
    var cubeNode2 = new CubeNode(0.1f, UIColor.Green);
    cubeNode2.Position = new SCNVector3(0.1f, 0, 0);

    // 50cm (0.5m)
    var cubeNode3
      = new CubeNode(0.5f, UIColor.Orange);
    cubeNode3.Position = new SCNVector3(0.5f, 0, 0);

    // 100cm (1m)
    var cubeNode4 = new CubeNode(1f, UIColor.Yellow);
    cubeNode4.Position = new SCNVector3(1.5f, 0, 0);

    this.sceneView.Scene.RootNode
        .AddChildNode(cubeNode1);
    this.sceneView.Scene.RootNode
        .AddChildNode(cubeNode2);
```

```
    this.sceneView.Scene.RootNode
        .AddChildNode(cubeNode3);
    this.sceneView.Scene.RootNode
        .AddChildNode(cubeNode4);
}
```

***Listing 2-5.*** CubeNode class

```
public class CubeNode : SCNNode
{
    public CubeNode(float size, UIColor color)
    {
        var material = new SCNMaterial();
        material.Diffuse.Contents = color;

        var geometry = SCNBox.Create(size, size, size,0);
        geometry.Materials = new[] { material };

        var rootNode = new SCNNode();
        rootNode.Geometry = geometry;

        AddChildNode(rootNode);
    }
}
```

# Configuration

When you start an ARSession with ARSession.Run(), you provide an instance of ARConfiguration. The sort of capabilities you want your AR app to have and how you want it to behave will determine the type of configuration you use.

For example, if you want to do face detection, you pass it an instance of ARFaceTrackingConfiguration along with some configuration variable such as the number of faces to track.

Here is a list of the configurations we will look at later in this book.

- ARWorldTrackingConfiguration enables world tracking including plane, image, and object detection, and we use it in the majority of examples in this book.

- `ARFaceTrackingConfiguration` enables face tracking, and we will look at this in Chapter 11, "Face Tracking and Expression Detection."

- `ARBodyTrackingConfiguration` enables body tracking, and we will look at this in Chapter 16, "Body Tracking."

# Summary

You should now have a good understanding of the basic concepts of what is necessary to start an Augmented Reality Session to set up your AR scene and understand how to find your way around the scene once it is running including sizing and the axis, coordinates, and positioning system.

In the next chapter, we will look at the kinds of things you can place in your scene including *Nodes, Geometries, Materials, and Anchors.*

# CHAPTER 3

# Nodes, Geometries, Materials, and Anchors

In this chapter, we will look at the building blocks that go together to create everything we can see and interact with in our Augmented Reality experiences. Let's start adding things to our AR scenes.

## Nodes

In your AR scene, you are almost certainly going to have one or more nodes (instances of SCNNode). By default, these nodes do not have any shape or form, so therefore don't look like anything. We give them form by applying a geometry and a visual appearance by applying materials to that geometry.

What might you use a node for you wonder? Well, almost everything. It may be as simple as placing a colored 3D sphere or a 2D plane showing an image into a scene, for example. Both of those items will be nodes.

We can specify the position of a node using SCNVector3 as we saw in Chapter 2, "Basic Concepts"; otherwise, its default position will be the WorldOrigin (0,0,0) when added to a scene.

A node can have many child nodes, and those child nodes have child nodes of their own, and so on. Why might you want to have child nodes you wonder? Well, if you placed 50 nodes in a scene and then want to change the position of all 50 nodes, you would have to change the position of each node in turn. Unless that is, you create a single node, then add those 50 nodes as children of that node, then you need only change the position of the parent node and the relative position of the child nodes will more accordingly.

L. Englestone, *.NET Developer's Guide to Augmented Reality in iOS*,
https://doi.org/10.1007/978-1-4842-6770-7_3

I like to think of nodes like Lego bricks, each individual piece with its own shape, size, appearance, and function, which by themselves aren't useful, but by putting them together, we can make something greater, something far more complex and useful.

# Opacity

It is possible to set several properties on a node including `Opacity`, which is something I love to use, even if just subtly. By changing a node's opacity, we are able to make it more or less opaque and conversely therefore more or less transparent.

Opacity is a float value that ranges from 0f (completely transparent) to 1f (completely opaque), and by default, a node's opacity value will be 1f (completely opaque).

In Listing 3-1, you can see how we can declare a new material (`SCNMaterial`), in this case a solid blue color. Then we create a new Geometry (a type of 2D or 3D shape), in this case a box (`SCNBox`) which is 1m in height, width, and depth and assign the material to the box, making a blue box. Then we create a new node (`SCNNode`) and set its geometry to be the new box. After which, we are setting the node's `opacity` to 0.5f, effectively making it 50% opaque. Then finally we add the node to the scene by calling `this.sceneView.Scene.RootNode.AddChildNode()`.

***Listing 3-1.*** Creating a simple node with shape, size, and color

```
// Create the Material
var material = new SCNMaterial();
material.Diffuse.Contents = UIColor.Blue;

// Create the Box Geometry and set its Material
var geometry = SCNBox.Create(1f, 1f, 1f, 0);
geometry.Materials = new[] { material };

// Create the Node and set its Geometry
var cubeNode = new SCNNode();
cubeNode.Geometry = geometry;

// Make the cube 50% opaque
cubeNode.Opacity = 0.5f;
```

```
// Add the Node to the Scene
// Remember, as we are not explicitly setting a position,
// The Node will appear at the WorldOrigin (0,0,0)
this.sceneView.Scene.RootNode.AddChildNode(cubeNode);
```

Worry not, Materials and Geometries are discussed in the upcoming sections.

# Geometries

The geometry is the shape or mesh that a node can have, and without them, our scenes would be very boring; indeed, as without them, we would just have a bunch of invisible formless nodes. Geometries can be simple shapes or complex meshes. In the following section, you can see the different types of basic built-in geometry shapes available for us to use.

# Built-in Geometry Shapes

There are a number of built-in geometry shapes that you can use for your nodes. But don't worry. You aren't limited by these basic shapes; you can provide a custom geometry or build a 3D model in another tool and import it into your app, something we will discuss in Chapter 13, "3D Models."

The following code in Listing 3-2 creates a simple box geometry for the node which is 10 cm in width, height, and depth which is then given a red material before being added to the scene.

***Listing 3-2.*** Creating a simple 10 cm red cube

```
var material = new SCNMaterial();
material.Diffuse.Contents = UIColor.Red;

var boxNode = new SCNNode();
boxNode.Geometry = SCNBox.Create(0.1f, 0.1f, 0.1f, 0);
boxNode.Geometry.Materials = new SCNMaterial[] { material };
this.sceneView.Scene.RootNode.AddChildNode(boxNode);
```

Here are the built-in geometry shapes we can use:

- **SCNPlane** – This is a 2D four-sided rectangle or square; they can be very useful for placing images onto show images in a scene or as surfaces on which to place other objects. It's worth noting that you can adjust the CornerRadius property of a plane to turn those sharp corners into softer, rounder corners.

- **SCNBox** – If you choose to use the same value for width, depth, and height, your box will be like a regular cube, or by using different values, it may be more like a flatter postal package. Similar to a SCNPlane, you can change your sharp box corners into softer, rounder corners, but this time by changing the box's ChamferRadius property.

- **SCNSphere** – A sphere, useful for depicting things like planets.

- **SCNCylinder** – A solid cylindrical shape.

- **SCNTorus** – A Torus is just a fancy word for a doughnut or ring shape.

- **SCNCone** – A solid cone shape with a circular base at one end and a point at the other.

- **SCNTube** – Similar to the SCNCylinder, except this is a hollow tube, like a pipe.

- **SCNText** – 3D text you can place in the scene, as like most text, you are able to set its Font and Size.

- **SCNPyramid** – Just like the Egyptians built, well kind of.

Each geometry requires a different set of parameters when calling its .Create() method to define different aspects of the shape. For example, SCNSphere.Create() only takes one parameter which is the radius of the sphere, whereas SCNBox.Create() takes three to define its width, height, and depth.

Figure 3-1 shows the aforementioned different types of geometry shapes we can use.

But even after creating a geometry and assigning it to a node, you won't be able to see it until you create and assign a material to it. So we had best look at how to use materials.

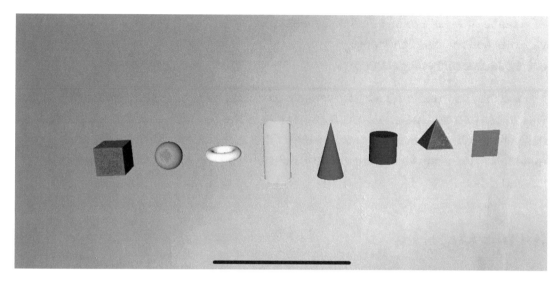

*Figure 3-1.* *The different types of built-in geometries*

# Materials

You apply one or more materials (instances of SCNMaterial) to a geometry to give it a visual appearance. We will specifically be looking at how to give an item a solid color or wrap it in an image.

## Solid Color Material

One of the most basic materials you can give a geometry is a solid color as shown in Listing 3-3 where we set the Contents property of the Material's Diffuse property to be UIColor.Red.

*Listing 3-3.* Setting a material to be a solid color

```
// Create the Material
var material = new SCNMaterial();
material.Diffuse.Contents = UIColor.Red;

// Create the Box Geometry and set its Material
var geometry = SCNBox.Create(1f, 1f, 1f, 0);
geometry.Materials = new[] { material };
```

```
// Create the Node and set its Geometry
var cubeNode = new SCNNode();
cubeNode.Geometry = geometry;
```

You may be wondering why a geometry accepts an array of materials; this is because we can use different materials on different sides of the geometry. For example, if we declared six different materials each using a different color and provided those six materials in the array for a box geometry, then we would get a box with six different-colored sides.

# Image Material

Another type of material you can give a geometry is an image. This can be useful if we want to wrap a geometry in an image or place an image on a 2D plane. Notice this time, we are setting a UIImage to the Materials Diffuse Contents property as shown in Listing 3-4. This Contents property accepts a few different types including UIColor and UIImage as we have already seen.

**Listing 3-4.** Setting a material to be an image

```
// Load the image
var image = UIImage.FromFile("Images/pineapple.jpg");

// Create the Material
var material = new SCNMaterial();
material.Diffuse.Contents = image;
material.DoubleSided = true;

// Create the Plane Geometry and set its Material
var geometry = SCNPlane.Create(1f, 1f);
geometry.Materials = new[] { material };

// Create the Node and set its Geometry
var rootNode = new SCNNode();
rootNode.Geometry = geometry;

// Add the Node to the Scene
this.sceneView.Scene.RootNode.AddChildNode(rootNode);
```

**Hint**    If you do not use `material.DoubleSided` = `true`, then your geometry may only be visible when viewed from certain angles.

It is worth mentioning that PNG images containing transparency can be used as well and the transparency will be maintained. For example, if you created a transparent PNG that contained some text and used that image as a material on a `SCNPlane`, you would just see floating text. This is quite a useful and nice effect.

# Material Fill Mode

By default, the fill mode of a material is solid. However, you can always change the fill mode to lines to see a kind of mesh that makes up the shape. In Listing 3-5 and Figure 3-2, you can see how the fill mode of the sphere geometry can be solid or lines.

*Listing 3-5.* Material fill modes

```
var material = new SCNMaterial();
material.Diffuse.Contents = colour;
material.FillMode = SCNFillMode.Lines;
```

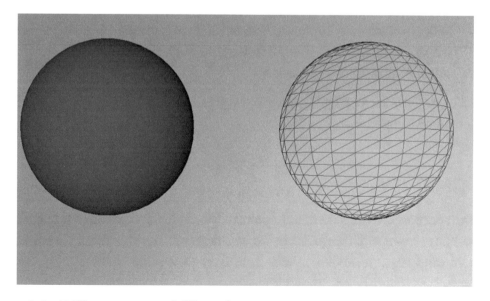

*Figure 3-2.* *Different material fill modes*

# Anchors

Anchors are points of reference that are either automatically detected or manually placed in the scene. For example, when doing image detection like we do in Chapter 10, "Image Detection," an ImageAnchor is automatically placed in the scene at the location of the detected image. They help tether our virtual objects to the real world.

The kinds of Anchors we will use in this book include

- **ARPlaneAnchor** – Represents a detected horizontal or vertical plane in a scene which we will use in Chapter 9, "Plane Detection," to help visualize walls, floors, and surfaces.

- **ARImageAnchor** – Represents a detected image in a scene which we will use in Chapter 10, "Image Detection," when detecting predefined images in a scene.

- **ARFaceAnchor** – Represents a detected face in a scene which we will use in Chapter 11, "Face Tracking and Expression Detection," where we can add other nodes to the detected face geometry and even detect a range of facial expressions.

- **ARObjectAnchor** – Represents a detected object in a scene which we will use in Chapter 15, "Object Detection," when the shape of a predefined "scanned" 3D object is detected in the scene.

- **ARBodyAnchor** – Represents a detected body in a scene which we will use in Chapter 16, "Body Tracking," to track the location and orientation of a body in the scene.

Anchors are crucial for keeping track of the presence and locations of points of interest to our AR experience.

# Things to Try

Using the concepts discussed in this chapter such as nodes, geometries, and materials and combining them with things discussed in Chapter 2, "Basic Concepts," such as positioning and sizes, you should now be able to try a few things yourself.

Here are some ideas to get you started.

**Create a snowman out of basic geometries and materials.**

Start by creating a single node and then adding other nodes with basic geometries to it with different positions, sizes, and materials to create a basic snowman. You could start with white spheres for the body and head, black spheres for eyes, brown spheres for buttons, and black cylinders for the hat.

**See how many items you can place in the scene and in different places.**

Now that you know how to place items in different places, see how many you can place in the scene at different positions with a large for or do while loop. You could even use Random, to place them at random positions.

**Place items of different sizes in the scene.**

Get a feel for how large a virtual 1 cm, 10 cm, and 1 m item is when placed in your scene.

**Place items of different colors and opacities in the scene.**

Using different colored materials, create different colored nodes, and see what they look like with different opacity values.

**Create transparent PNGs and use them as a geometries material.**

Create a transparent PNG, add some large thick text to it and use that image as the material of a SCNPlane, see how effective it is using transparent PNGs in this manner.

**See how big or small you can make nodes.**

See how small an item you can place in the scene and still see it; then see how large an item you can place in a scene (for the latter, you may need to place it far away from you; else, you run the risk of being *inside* the item, if you occupy the same space as it).

# Summary

We've discussed nodes which are the physical building blocks of Augmented Reality in ARKit that we will use a great deal, how to make use of built-in geometry shapes, how to give them a visual appearance, and how to place them in the scene.

In the next chapter, we will look at some of the *built-in tools and guides* we can use to help develop and understand our Augmented Reality scenes.

# CHAPTER 4

# Built-in AR Guides

ARKit comes with a few useful built-in guides and tools that can help when developing your first Augmented Reality experiences. We can enable some of these by setting their flag in the SCNDebugOptions when setting up our scene.

## Show Feature Points

Toggling on the flag to show feature points is something I recommend you do when creating your first app. It helps show you how dependent the app and camera are on lighting conditions and surfaces. However, in later apps, you will seldom need to turn this feature on.

You enable it by setting a DebugOptions flag as shown in Listing 4-1.

***Listing 4-1.*** Enabling feature points in the code

```
public ViewController(IntPtr handle) : base(handle)
{
    this.sceneView = new ARSCNView
    {
        DebugOptions = ARSCNDebugOptions.ShowFeaturePoints
    };

    this.View.AddSubview(this.sceneView);
}
```

When the ShowFeaturePoints DebugOption is enabled, you will see yellow dots appearing on surfaces within your scene like those shown in Figure 4-1. An abundance of feature points means that ARKit can detect many feature points in the scene. This is good because ARKit uses feature points to help maintain the position of virtual objects in a scene.

© Lee Englestone 2021
L. Englestone, *.NET Developer's Guide to Augmented Reality in iOS,*
https://doi.org/10.1007/978-1-4842-6770-7_4

You will notice that when turning ShowFeaturePoints on and running your app in a poorly lit environment or against featureless surfaces (such as plain walls or glass surfaces), there will be far fewer yellow dots. This helps confirm that in order for your app to run optimally, it should be used in a well-lit, feature-filled environment.

***Figure 4-1.*** *Showing feature points in a scene helps us understand how the app is looking for points of interest in the scene*

## Show World Origin and Coordinate Axis

As briefly mentioned when we introduced the concept of position in Chapter 2, "Basic Concepts," it is possible to turn on a guide which shows the X, Y, and Z coordinate axes at the world origin as shown in Listing 4-2. This can help us orient ourselves, reminding us which direction the X, Y, and Z axes are as seen in Figure 4-2.

As the axis is shown at the world origin, it indicates the location of the device when the session started, where position 0,0,0 is. Remember a node added to the scene that hasn't been given a specific location will appear at the world origin.

***Listing 4-2.*** Enabling WorldOrigin helper

```
public ViewController(IntPtr handle) : base(handle)
{
    this.sceneView = new ARSCNView
    {
        DebugOptions = ARSCNDebugOptions.ShowWorldOrigin
    };

    this.View.AddSubview(this.sceneView);
}
```

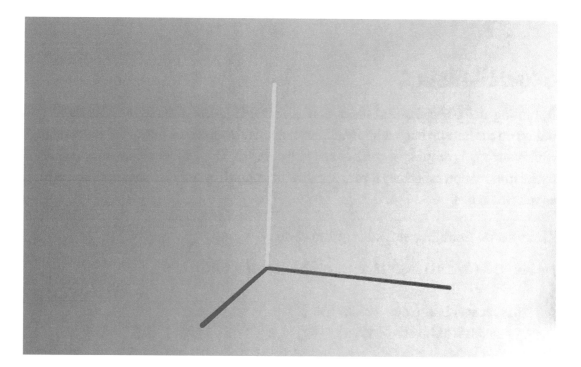

***Figure 4-2.***  *Showing coordinate axis at the WorldOrigin*

Note that you can enable multiple debug options at the same time. For example, in Listing 4-3, you can see that we are showing both feature points and the world origin/axis in the scene.

***Listing 4-3.*** Enabling multiple debug options

```
public ViewController(IntPtr handle) : base(handle)
{
    this.sceneView = new ARSCNView
    {
        DebugOptions
        = ARSCNDebugOptions.ShowFeaturePoints |
          ARSCNDebugOptions.ShowWorldOrigin
    };

    this.View.AddSubview(this.sceneView);
}
```

# Show Statistics

By turning on the ShowStatistics option as shown in Listing 4-4 and pressing the + button on the bottom bar, additional information is shown at the bottom of the screen while your app is running as can be seen in Figure 4-3. The statistics view shows some useful information especially if your app is a bit sluggish or not performing as smoothly as you would like.

***Listing 4-4.*** Enabling Statistics in the code

```
public ViewController(IntPtr handle) : base(handle)
{
    this.sceneView = new ARSCNView {
        ShowsStatistics = true
    };

    this.View.AddSubview(this.sceneView);
}
```

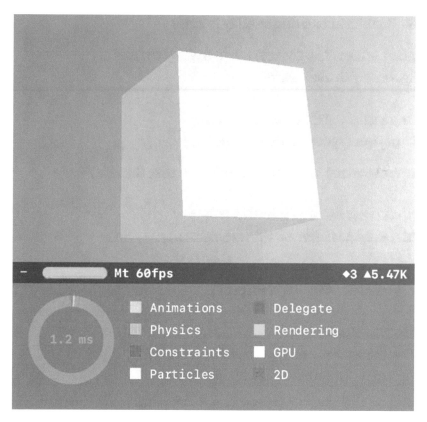

**Figure 4-3.** *Showing Statistics gives information about how much effort the scene is taking to render*

The statistics view shows the framerate as frames per second (fps) as well as the GPU usage of the view. You will want to keep an eye on the fps if it starts dropping too low; 60 fps is the maximum, and values above 30 are acceptable. It also shows the number of Nodes (diamond) and number of Polygons (triangle) on the scene. If your app is starting to suffer from performance problems, you may want to show statistics to investigate what might be causing the slowdown.

# Coaching Overlay

As it is important for your app to understand its surroundings to function and place things accurately in your scene, to help with this, you can use a built-in coaching overlay which encourages the user to move their camera around until the app has gathered sufficient information to be able to understand the scene accurately. You can add a coaching overlay to your app as shown in Listing 4-5.

***Listing 4-5.***  Enabling coaching overlay in code

```
public partial class ViewController : UIViewController,
IARCoachingOverlayViewDelegate
{
    private readonly ARSCNView sceneView;
    ARCoachingOverlayView coachingOverlay;

    public ViewController(IntPtr handle) : base(handle)
    {
        this.sceneView = new ARSCNView();
        this.View.AddSubview(this.sceneView);
    }

    public override void ViewDidLoad()
    {
        base.ViewDidLoad();
        this.sceneView.Frame = this.View.Frame;
    }

    public override void ViewDidAppear(bool animated)
    {
        base.ViewDidAppear(animated);

        this.sceneView.Session.Run(new
            ARWorldTrackingConfiguration {
            PlaneDetection = ARPlaneDetection.Horizontal,
        });

        coachingOverlay = new ARCoachingOverlayView();
        coachingOverlay.Session = sceneView.Session;
        coachingOverlay.Delegate = this;
        coachingOverlay.ActivatesAutomatically = true;
        coachingOverlay.Goal = ARCoachingGoal.HorizontalPlane;
        coachingOverlay.TranslatesAutoresizingMaskIntoConstraints = false;

        sceneView.AddSubview(coachingOverlay);
```

```
        // Keeps the coaching overlay in the center of the screen
        var layoutConstraints = new NSLayoutConstraint[]
        {
            coachingOverlay.CenterXAnchor.ConstraintEqualTo(
                View.CenterXAnchor),
            coachingOverlay.CenterYAnchor.ConstraintEqualTo(
                View.CenterYAnchor),
            coachingOverlay.WidthAnchor.ConstraintEqualTo(
                View.WidthAnchor),
            coachingOverlay.HeightAnchor.ConstraintEqualTo(
                View.HeightAnchor),
        };

        NSLayoutConstraint.ActivateConstraints(
            layoutConstraints);
    }

    public override void ViewDidDisappear(bool animated)
    {
        base.ViewDidDisappear(animated);
        this.sceneView.Session.Pause();
    }

    public override void DidReceiveMemoryWarning()
    {
        base.DidReceiveMemoryWarning();
    }
}
```

The result can be seen in Figure 4-4; a transparent animated image overlays the screen encouraging the user to move the phone around; after it understands the scene sufficiently, it disappears.

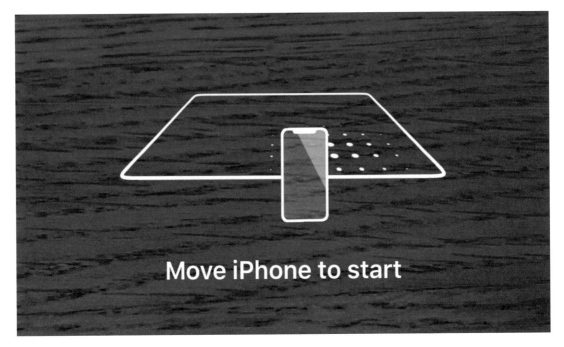

*Figure 4-4.* *Coaching overlays can help guide users to achieve a goal (such as detect a plane)*

## Summary

Some of these built-in guides can be useful when first starting out creating and familiarizing yourself with Augmented Reality experiences, but when you come to publishing and distributing your app, you will almost certainly want to disable them.

In the next chapter, we will look at one of my favorite and impressive features for creating engaging experiences which is *Animations* which are crucial to give your experience a dynamic feel.

# CHAPTER 5

# Animations

An easy way of making your Augmented Reality apps look impressive is by adding a little bit of movement to it by animating one or more nodes. Otherwise, it can look a bit static and artificial. This may be as simple as fading nodes in and out or animating their position or size, and fortunately, it is easy to do.

Technically, in SceneKit, we will be using something called a *SCNAction*. But because the actions we will look at are enabling our animations, I will refer to SCNActions as animations in this chapter.

## Animating Opacity

By animating the opacity of one or more objects in the Scene, nice effects like fading in and fading out their appearance can be achieved. Listing 5-1 shows how to animate the opacity of a node from 0f (zero opacity) to 1f (full opacity).

***Listing 5-1.*** Fading in a node from 0% opacity to 100% opacity over 3 seconds

```
var material = new SCNMaterial();
material.Diffuse.Contents = UIColor.Blue;

var geometry = SCNSphere.Create(0.5f);
geometry.Materials = new[] { material };

var opacityAction = SCNAction.FadeOpacityTo(1f, 3);
var sphereNode = new SCNNode();
sphereNode.Geometry = geometry;
sphereNode.Opacity = 0f;
sphereNode.RunAction(opacityAction);
this.sceneView.Scene.RootNode.AddChildNode(sphereNode);
```

© Lee Englestone 2021
L. Englestone, *.NET Developer's Guide to Augmented Reality in iOS*,
https://doi.org/10.1007/978-1-4842-6770-7_5

Animating an item into the scene is a great way to introduce items into your virtual environment as can be seen in Figure 5-1. It feels a lot more natural than something suddenly appearing in the blink of an eye.

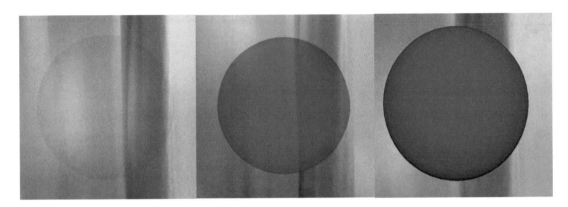

***Figure 5-1.** Changing the opacity from 0f to 1f over 3 seconds*

# Animating Scale

While animating an object's scale (size) is possible, I recommend that only minor, subtle changes in scale be used to achieve the required effect. It is possible to animate an object's scale in its X, Y, and Z axis (or all) directions. Listing 5-2 shows how to scale a nodes size to 10% of its original size over a second.

***Listing 5-2.** Decreasing a nodes size by 90% over a second*

```
var material = new SCNMaterial();
material.Diffuse.Contents = UIColor.Yellow;

var geometry = SCNSphere.Create(0.2f);
geometry.Materials = new[] { material };

var scaleAction = SCNAction.ScaleBy(0.1f, 1);
var sphereNode = new SCNNode();
sphereNode.Geometry = geometry;
sphereNode.RunAction(scaleAction);
this.sceneView.Scene.RootNode.AddChildNode(sphereNode);
```

And Figure 5-2 shows the shrinking sphere animation.

*Figure 5-2.* *Changing the scale of a node to 10% of its original size over 1 second*

# Animating Position

It is possible to animate the position of a node from one position to another and this can be achieved using the code in Listing 5-3. You may want to use this animation to make a node move closer or further away from you.

*Listing 5-3.* Moving a node's position 0.5 meter in the Y axis over 3 seconds

```
var material = new SCNMaterial();
material.Diffuse.Contents = UIColor.Blue;

var geometry = SCNSphere.Create(0.5f);
geometry.Materials = new[] { material };

var positionAction = SCNAction.MoveBy(new SCNVector3(0, 0.5f, 0f), 3);
var sphereNode = new SCNNode();
sphereNode.Geometry = geometry;
sphereNode.RunAction(positionAction);
this.sceneView.Scene.RootNode.AddChildNode(sphereNode);
```

Animating the position of our nodes helps us change them from being boring static objects in our scene to dynamic moving objects.

# Animating Orientation

Want to rotate a node? Either by a few degrees or to make it spin? Well, you can, as shown in Listing 5-4. Rotating objects in our scene can help show that they have certain degrees of freedom and not completely static.

51

***Listing 5-4.*** Rotating a node by 360 degrees over 3 seconds

```
var material = new SCNMaterial();
material.Diffuse.Contents = UIColor.Green;

var geometry = SCNBox.Create(0.1f, 0.1f, 0.1f, 0);
geometry.Materials = new[] { material };

var rotateAction = SCNAction.RotateBy(
    0, (float)(Math.PI), 0, 3);

var cubeNode = new SCNNode();
cubeNode.RunAction(rotateAction);
this.sceneView.Scene.RootNode.AddChildNode(cubeNode);
```

The result is a slowly spinning cube as shown in Figure 5-3.

***Figure 5-3.*** *Rotating a cube by 360 degrees over 3 seconds*

## Repeat Behavior

In the previous examples, the animations will by default run once. If you wish, it is easy to make them run a predefined number of times as shown in Listing 5-5 or repeatedly as shown in Listing 5-6.

***Listing 5-5.*** Repeating a rotate action five times

```
var rotateAction = SCNAction.RotateBy(
    0, (float)(Math.PI), 0, 3);
```

```
var repeatRotationFiveTimes =
   SCNAction.RepeatAction(rotateAction, 5);

sphereNode.RunAction(repeatRotationFiveTimes);
```

***Listing 5-6.*** Repeating a rotate action indefinitely

```
var rotateAction = SCNAction.RotateBy(
   0, (float)(Math.PI), 0, 3);

var repeatRotationForever =
   SCNAction.RepeatActionForever(rotateAction);

sphereNode.RunAction(repeatRotationForever);
```

# Animation Easing

I like to liken easing to acceleration and deceleration when driving a car. From a stand still, it takes some time to get to your desired speed and some time to slow the car to a stop as well. That is easing. The animation is happening at different speeds at different times. The alternative to easing is Linear animation where the speed of the animation is constant from beginning to end. Listing 5-7 shows how to use easing in your animations.

You may wonder when you may want to use easing. Personally, I think it gives animations a more "natural" look than the default Linear. The options for easing are `EaseIn`, `EaseOut`, `EaseInEaseOut`, and `Linear`.

***Listing 5-7.*** Easing animations can make them look more natural than their linear counterparts

```
var opacityAction = SCNAction.FadeOpacityTo(1f, 3);
opacityAction.TimingMode = SCNActionTimingMode.EaseInEaseOut;
sphereNode.Opacity = 0f;
sphereNode.RunAction(opacityAction);
```

# Combining Animations

To create even more interesting animations, you can combine them in a couple of ways. For example, you could fade in a node while you move it toward you (along the Z axis) while making it grow (scale up).

And you can either combine these animations so that they happen simultaneously or in sequence as shown in Listing 5-8.

***Listing 5-8.*** You can group animations to play simultaneously or sequentially

```
var opacityAction = SCNAction.FadeOpacityTo(1f, 1);
var scaleAction = SCNAction.ScaleBy(1.2f, 1);
var positionAction = SCNAction.MoveBy(
   new SCNVector3(0, 0, -0.1f), 1);

// Would run the actions all at the same time
var simultaneousActions = SCNAction.Group(new SCNAction[] {
      opacityAction, scaleAction, positionAction });

sphereNode.RunAction(simultaneousActions);

// Would run the actions one after another
var sequentialActions = SCNAction.Sequence(new SCNAction[] {
     opacityAction, scaleAction, positionAction });

sphereNode.RunAction(sequentialActions);
```

*Because SCNAction.Group() and SCNAction.Sequence() return SCNAction, you can go on to group or sequence those groups and sequences into "other" groups and sequences.*

# Waiting

If you want to wait a little before or between animations, you can use SCNAction. Wait(numberOfSeconds) to put a delay into your sequence of animations. The code for this is simple as shown in Listing 5-9.

**Listing 5-9.** You can use wait actions to have even greater control over the timing of your animations

```
var waitAction = SCNAction.Wait(1);
```

# Summary

So by now your mind should be racing with ways of moving, scaling, and fading nodes in your scene to create engaging, dynamic, and interesting AR experiences. Just bear in mind that while animations are powerful when used subtly, too many animations can be easily overwhelming. It's up to you to learn how to strike a balance.

In the next chapter, we will look at *Constraints* which can make it easier to get nodes to behave in particular ways. Sounds cryptic, right? Well, turn the page and let's look at what constraints can do for us.

# CHAPTER 6

# Constraints

Using constraints on our nodes allows us to restrict their behavior in a certain way. Using them, you can make nodes, for example, always face the camera or always face another node if you wish.

## BillboardConstraint

I presume this effect is named after the experience you have as a passenger in a car when you look at a billboard as you go past it.

If you apply this constraint to a node, it always faces the camera. If you are wondering why you might ever need this, imagine if you have a sign or a label providing information that you want the user to always be able to see. That would be a good use case for the SCNBillboardConstraint. As you can see from Listing 6-1, adding a constraint to a node is very simple.

*Listing 6-1.* Have a node always face the camera using a SCNBillboardConstraint

```
var rootNode = new SCNNode
{
    Geometry = CreateGeometry(),
    Constraints = new[] { new SCNBillboardConstraint() }
};
```

## LookAtConstraint

The LookAtConstraint is similar to the BillboardConstraint in some ways; however, this constraint tells the node to always look at (face) a particular node.

© Lee Englestone 2021
L. Englestone, *.NET Developer's Guide to Augmented Reality in iOS*,
https://doi.org/10.1007/978-1-4842-6770-7_6

Previously, I have used this to make a number of surrounding nodes "look at" a center invisible node with great effect as can be seen in Figure 6-1.

***Figure 6-1.*** *You can use LookAtConstraints to point nodes to look at other nodes*

This effect is achieved using the code shown in Listing 6-2.

***Listing 6-2.*** Use "SCNLookAtConstraint" to make nodes always face another node

```
var lookAtConstraint = SCNLookAtConstraint.Create(targetNode);
lookAtConstraint.GimbalLockEnabled = true;
imagePlaneNode.Constraints = new SCNConstraint[]
{
    lookAtConstraint
};
```

Using `GimbalLockEnabled=true` stops the node from rotating horizontally if the camera is rotated.

# Other Constraints

There are a number of other, more advanced constraints that we can use from SceneKit; however, they are beyond the scope of this introductory book. They include

- SCNOrientationConstraint

- SCNTransformConstraint

- SCNDistanceConstraint

- SCNAvoidOccluderConstraint

- SCNAccelerationConstraint

- SCNSliderConstraint

- SCNReplicatorConstraint

- SCNIKConstraint

# Things to Try

**Play with LookAtConstraint**.
Place a node with no geometry (therefore invisible) at the WorldOrigin. Add multiple 2D planes to a scene whose nodes have a SCNLookAtConstraint set to look at the world origin node.

**Play with Billboard Constraint**.
Add multiple 2D planes into a scene whose nodes have a SCNBillboardConstraint and notice how they always face the camera.

# Summary

The SCNBillboardConstraint and SCNLookAtConstraint constraints are useful ways of restricting how you want your nodes to behave and are especially useful as they mean you don't need to use complex maths to calculate the exact angles necessary to achieve the same effect.

In the next chapter, we will look at Lighting, something that at first glance may not seem all that important but actually can make an AR experience a lot better or a lot worse if not factored into your AR experiences.

# CHAPTER 7

# Lighting

It turns out that lighting is extremely important when it comes to making our AR scenes look realistic. For example, if it is a bright day but we place a dark object in the scene, it looks very artificial; conversely, the same can be said for placing a very light object in a dark environment. So where possible we want to take the real-world lighting conditions into consideration in our scene.

Another consideration for creating realistic AR experiences is shadows.

If you are placing objects in your scene between a light source (such as the sun) and a surface (such as the floor), your mind expects to see a shadow. We can create these fake shadows to make our scenes look like they would in the real world.

## Automatically Add Default Lighting

By default, "default" lighting is added to your SceneView as the default value of `ARSCNView.AutoenablesDefaultLighting` is true. This places an omnidirectional light source in the scene that points in the same direction as the camera. This may be fine for your initial AR creations, but if you want more control over specific lighting instances, you may wish to turn this off by setting `AutoenablesDefaultLighting=false`.

## Automatically Update Default Lighting

We can add default lighting to the scene that tries to mimic real-world lighting conditions using the `ARSCNView.AutomaticallyUpdatesLighting` property. So if the real-world lighting changes, the artificial light changes as well. Again, this is true by default, and if you wish to have more control over lighting in your scenes, you can set `AutomaticallyUpdatesLighting=false` as shown in Listing 7-1.

© Lee Englestone 2021
L. Englestone, *.NET Developer's Guide to Augmented Reality in iOS*,
https://doi.org/10.1007/978-1-4842-6770-7_7

***Listing 7-1.*** A default light source is added to the scene, but you can turn it off if you want to have more control/add your own light sources

```
public ViewController(IntPtr handle) : base(handle)
{
    this.sceneView = new ARSCNView
    {
        AutoenablesDefaultLighting = false,
        AutomaticallyUpdatesLighting = false
    };

    this.View.AddSubview(this.sceneView);
}
```

# Light Types

Rather than solely relying on default lighting, it is possible to place one or more specific light sources in a scene by adding an instance of SCNLight to a SCNNode.

These are the different types of light sources (SCNLight.Type) you can use:

- **Ambient** – Emits light uniformly in all directions.

- **Directional** – Emits light in a certain direction with uniform strength, so its originating position doesn't matter. It will look the same whether placed 10 cm or 1 m away.

- **Omni** – Similar to a directional, however, its position can dictate the strength of the light. Use this if the distance of the light source matters in your scene.

- **Spot** – Similar to Omni but the strength of the light gradually falls off forming a cone of light.

In the real world, light bounces off multiple surfaces to light an area. The nearest thing we can do to mimic this is adding an Ambient light source. Then to better represent some actual light sources, we can use Directional lights. So it is not uncommon to add multiple types of light sources to your scene.

The example in Listing 7-2 shows a directional light being added to a SCNNode and made to point straight down, effectively lighting the top of any node placed underneath it.

***Listing 7-2.*** You create a light source and add it to a SCNNode

```
var light = SCNLight.Create();
light.LightType = SCNLightType.Directional;
light.Intensity = 2000f;
light.ShadowColor = UIColor.Black.ColorWithAlpha(0.5f);
light.ShadowRadius = 4;
light.ShadowSampleCount = 4;
light.CastsShadow = true;

var lightNode = new SCNNode();
lightNode.Light = light;
lightNode.EulerAngles = new SCNVector3((float)-Math.PI / 2, 0, 0);
```

---

**Note**    If the only virtual light source in your scene is a directional light, any surfaces that are parallel to light direction will be black.

---

If we wanted, we can then do something clever and place this light above other nodes in our scene to roughly mimic the sun and cast shadows on a plane placed on the ground as can be seen in the next section.

# Adding Shadows

Making it look like your objects are casting a shadow in a scene is as simple as adding a light source (SCNLight) above the object and a transparent plane below the object to act as a surface on which the shadow to fall as can be seen in Figure 7-1.

***Figure 7-1.*** *A virtual shadow shown on a virtual plane underneath a virtual cube cast by a virtual light source*

The experience with and without the shadow are miles apart. Without the shadow, the virtual cube still appears to be present in the scene, but our only way of understanding its position and how high it is above the floor is by moving around. However, including the shadow instantly gives us a much clearer indication as to the position of the cube and its height above the floor.

In Listing 7-3, because we want to include plane detection, we use an ARSCNViewDelegate, and this time, rather than have a separate class implement the IARSCNViewDelegate, we will have our ViewController implement it and set our Scene View Delegate to be the class itself (this).

In ViewDidAppear, we are enabling horizontal plane detection in the ARWorldTrackingConfiguration. We are also creating an instance of a directional light, setting its properties such as intensity, direction, and so on, then creating a SCNNode to *hold* the light, and then placing the node containing the light in the scene.

Then we are creating a cube shaped and adding it to the scene, making sure to position it *below* the light node.

Then in the DidUpdateNode method, we are making sure the material of the detected plane's lighting model is SCNLightingModel.ShadowOnly, effectively making it transparent for all but the casted shadow.

*Listing 7-3.* If you add a light source above other nodes in a scene, you can make them all cast a shadow, making the scene look more realistic

```
public partial class ViewController : UIViewController, IARSCNViewDelegate
    {
        private readonly ARSCNView sceneView;

        public ViewController(IntPtr handle) : base(handle)
        {
            this.sceneView = new ARSCNView
            {
                AutoenablesDefaultLighting = true,
                AutomaticallyUpdatesLighting = true,
                Delegate = this
            };

            this.View.AddSubview(this.sceneView);
        }

        public override void ViewDidLoad()
        {
            base.ViewDidLoad();
            this.sceneView.Frame = this.View.Frame;
        }

        public override void ViewDidAppear(bool animated)
        {
            base.ViewDidAppear(animated);

            var configuration
                = new ARWorldTrackingConfiguration
            {
                AutoFocusEnabled = true,
                PlaneDetection = ARPlaneDetection.Horizontal,
                LightEstimationEnabled = true,
```

```
            WorldAlignment = ARWorldAlignment.Gravity,
            EnvironmentTexturing =
                AREnvironmentTexturing.Automatic
        };

        this.sceneView.Session.Run(configuration);

        var light = SCNLight.Create();
        light.LightType = SCNLightType.Directional;
        light.Intensity = 2000f;
        light.ShadowColor =
            UIColor.Black.ColorWithAlpha(0.5f);
        light.ShadowRadius = 4;
        light.ShadowSampleCount = 4;
        light.CastsShadow = true;

        var lightNode = new SCNNode();
        lightNode.Light = light;
        lightNode.EulerAngles
            = new SCNVector3((float)-Math.PI / 2, 0, 0);

        var cube = SCNBox.Create(0.1f, 0.1f, 0.1f, 0.02f);
        var metal = SCNMaterial.Create();
        metal.LightingModelName =
            SCNLightingModel.PhysicallyBased;
        metal.Roughness.Contents = new NSNumber(0.1);
        metal.Metalness.Contents = new NSNumber(1);
        cube.FirstMaterial = metal;

        var cubeNode = new SCNNode();
        cubeNode.Geometry = cube;
        cubeNode.CastsShadow = true;

    this.sceneView.Scene.RootNode
        .AddChildNode(lightNode);

    this.sceneView.Scene.RootNode
        .AddChildNode(cubeNode);
      }
```

```
[Export("renderer:didUpdateNode:forAnchor:")]
public void DidUpdateNode(ISCNSceneRenderer renderer,
    SCNNode node, ARAnchor anchor)
{
    if (anchor is ARPlaneAnchor planeAnchor)
    {
        var plane =
            ARSCNPlaneGeometry.Create(sceneView.Device);
        plane.Update(planeAnchor.Geometry);
        plane.FirstMaterial.LightingModelName =
            SCNLightingModel.ShadowOnly;
        node.Geometry = plane;
        node.CastsShadow = false;
    }
}
}
```

Make sure if you are using the IARSCNViewDelegate on your ViewController class rather than a separate class that you decorate the DidUpdateNode method with [Export( "renderer:didUpdateNode:forAnchor:")] as shown in Listing 7-3. It is easy to forget, as I have many a time, and wondered why my shadows were not showing.

---

**Note**    If you can't see any shadows, make sure the nodes in your scene have their CastsShadow property set to true.

---

# Things to Try

**Experiment with different light source types and lighting properties.**

Try adding different light sources to your scene (along with a number of different shaped nodes) to see what effect they have on them. Try different light intensities and directions. Try enabling and disabling default automatic lighting to see the effect on your scene.

**Cast shadows.**

Make sure you can get an example working that casts a shadow, preferably with multiple objects, casting multiple shadows, as shadows really do make a scene pop and look more real.

# Summary

While you can create Augmented Reality experiences with little consideration for lighting and in fact let ARKit even add default lighting to your scenes, to get more realistic experiences, you will want to manually take control of lighting in your scenes yourself. Play around with different types of lighting with different strengths in different positions pointing in different directions.

As we have seen, adding artificial shadows adds an extra level of believability to our experiences as we expect objects in the real world to cast shadows, so it makes sense to get our virtual objects to cast shadows where possible.

In the next chapter, we will look at even more ways of engaging the user in our experiences, this time using Video and Sound.

# CHAPTER 8

# Video and Sound

To add another dimension of interaction to your Augmented Reality experience, you can incorporate sound and video to your scenes. It is especially effective when they are the result of interacting with items in the scene.

## Playing Sound

Playing sound is a very simple affair; you just use an instance of AVAudioPlayer, provide it with the location of a sound file (making sure you have added it to your project), and call .Play() as can be seen in Listing 8-1.

***Listing 8-1.*** Playing sound in an AR scene

```
NSUrl songURL = new NSUrl($"Sounds/sound.mp3");
NSError err;
AVAudioPlayer player
    = new AVAudioPlayer(songURL, "Song", out err);
player.Volume = 0.5f;
player.FinishedPlaying += delegate {
    player = null;
};
player.Play();
```

As sound is a great way of feeding back interaction with your app, if you wanted, you could play a sound when a SCNNode is pressed in a scene, for example. Or you could have sound play when your app first loads.

© Lee Englestone 2021
L. Englestone, *.NET Developer's Guide to Augmented Reality in iOS*,
https://doi.org/10.1007/978-1-4842-6770-7_8

# Playing Video

You have to see it to believe it, because it looks kind of awesome, but you can play videos inside your Augmented Reality scenes which appear almost like virtual TV screens or monitors.

In this example, we need to use a SKVideoNode and SKScene to play the video.

In Listing 8-2, you can see that we are placing the video on a 2D plane using a SCNMaterial. As this is a material, you could use it elsewhere, for example, on the sides of a 3D box.

***Listing 8-2.*** Playing video in an AR scene

```
public override void ViewDidAppear(bool animated)
{
    base.ViewDidAppear(animated);
    this.sceneView.Session.Run(new
        ARWorldTrackingConfiguration {
          LightEstimationEnabled = true,
          WorldAlignment = ARWorldAlignment.GravityAndHeading
        });
    var videoNode
      = new SKVideoNode("Videos/big-buck-bunny-wide.mp4");

    // Without this the video will be inverted upside down and
    // back to front
    videoNode.YScale = -1;
    videoNode.Play();

    var videoScene = new SKScene();
    videoScene.Size = new CoreGraphics.CGSize(640, 360);
    videoScene.ScaleMode = SKSceneScaleMode.AspectFill;
    videoNode.Position
      = new CoreGraphics.CGPoint(videoScene.Size.Width / 2,
          videoScene.Size.Height / 2);
    videoScene.AddChild(videoNode);

    // Set to be the same aspect ratio as the video itself
    //(1.77)
```

```
    var width = 0.5f;
    var length = 0.28f;

    var material = new SCNMaterial();
    material.Diffuse.Contents = videoScene;
    material.DoubleSided = true;

    var geometry = SCNPlane.Create(width, length);
    geometry.Materials = new[] { material };

    var planeNode = new SCNNode();
    planeNode.Geometry = geometry;
    planeNode.Position = new SCNVector3(0, 0, -0.5f);

    this.sceneView.Scene.RootNode.AddChildNode(planeNode);
}
```

In Listing 8-2, you will also notice that we must use a couple of more things from SceneKit to play a video, including SKScene and SKVideoNode.

In Figure 8-1, you can see how a floating 2D plane can show a video being played. It is even possible to alter its opacity to make it semitransparent or have it cast a shadow as discussed in Chapter 7, "Lighting."

***Figure 8-1.*** *Playing a video on a floating 2D plane*

# Things to Try

**Play numerous videos simultaneously.**

See if you can play the same video file on multiple plane nodes simultaneously; then see if you can play different video files simultaneously on different nodes.

See how many nodes you can do this with simultaneously. 5? 50?

**Play a video on a huge plane.**

Ever dreamt of an 80-inch TV? See if you can recreate that by playing a movie file on a huge 2D plane.

# Summary

Using sound in your Augmented Reality experiences can help provide auditory feedback when the user interacts with your app, and using videos can help engage, entertain, or communicate with your user. Both provide a greater level of engagement with the user.

In the next chapter, we will look at plane detection which identifies surfaces such as floors and walls. Once we have detected these surfaces, we can do some interesting things with them.

# CHAPTER 9

# Plane Detection

The ability to detect surfaces such as floors, walls, and surfaces is important as these dictate the limits of our scenes environment as well as enabling us to place things upon them.

The commercial applications of this AR feature are interesting. It is already used by some businesses to detect walls and place products such as wallpaper or pictures on them to allow customers to preview items in their homes before buying them.

## Detecting Planes

It is possible to set plane detection to just detect horizontal, vertical, or both horizontal and vertical planes.

During plane detection, as the camera is moved around and detects more of its environment, it can detect new planes or update its understanding of planes already detected.

When a new plane is detected, an `ARPlaneAnchor` is placed at the detected location. This anchor holds details about the detected plane such as its type (horizontal or vertical), position, orientation, width, and length and is automatically given a unique ID so that it can be distinguished from other planes.

Bear in mind that low lighting conditions and featureless or reflective surfaces will hinder ARKit's ability to detect planes. For example, ARKit will struggle to detect a plain white wall or a wall in a dimly lit room.

## Remembering Planes

It is often desired and useful to keep track of detected planes in your app. In Listing 9-2 as well as the code for detecting planes, you will see code for storing the detected planes in a variable for easy retrieval later on.

© Lee Englestone 2021
L. Englestone, *.NET Developer's Guide to Augmented Reality in iOS*,
https://doi.org/10.1007/978-1-4842-6770-7_9

# ARSCNViewDelegate (Scene View Delegate)

Generally speaking, it is common practice to create a dedicated class (an instance of `ARSCNViewDelegate`) that will handle events that are fired when different anchors are detected and placed in the scene, for example, when planes, images, or faces are detected. We will discuss this further in the chapters on Plane and Image detection as well as Face Tracking.

So in order to enable plane detection, you will need to set your SceneView's SceneViewDelegate as shown in Listings 9-1 and 9-2.

***Listing 9-1.*** Setting a Delegate for the `ARSCNView`

```
public ViewController(IntPtr handle) : base(handle)
{
    this.sceneView = new ARSCNView
    {
        AutoenablesDefaultLighting = true,
        Delegate = new SceneViewDelegate()
    };

    this.View.AddSubview(this.sceneView);
}
```

**Note**   Rather than use a separate class to act as the Scene View Delegate, it is possible to have your ViewController class implement `IARSCNViewDelegate` and set the Delegate to `this` (itself).

***Listing 9-2.*** The instance of ARSCNViewDelegate will detect and respond to events that are fired when new planes are detected or existing planes are updated

```
public class SceneViewDelegate : ARSCNViewDelegate
{
    private readonly IDictionary<NSUuid, PlaneNode> planeNodes = new
    Dictionary<NSUuid, PlaneNode>();
```

```csharp
public override void DidAddNode(
    ISCNSceneRenderer renderer,
     SCNNode node, ARAnchor anchor)
{
    if (anchor is ARPlaneAnchor planeAnchor)
    {
        UIColor colour;

        if(planeAnchor.Alignment == ARPlaneAnchorAlignment.Vertical) {
            colour = UIColor.Red;
        }
        else {
            colour = UIColor.Blue;
        }

        var planeNode = new PlaneNode(
            planeAnchor, colour);

        var angle = (float)(-Math.PI / 2);
        planeNode.EulerAngles
            = new SCNVector3(angle, 0, 0);

        node.AddChildNode(planeNode);
        this.planeNodes.Add(anchor.Identifier, planeNode);
    }
}

public override void DidRemoveNode(
    ISCNSceneRenderer renderer, SCNNode node,
    ARAnchor anchor)
{
    if (anchor is ARPlaneAnchor planeAnchor) {
        this.planeNodes[anchor.Identifier].RemoveFromParentNode();
        this.planeNodes.Remove(anchor.Identifier);
    }
}
```

```
public override void DidUpdateNode(ISCNSceneRenderer renderer,
    SCNNode node, ARAnchor anchor)
{
    if (anchor is ARPlaneAnchor planeAnchor) {
        this.planeNodes[anchor.Identifier]
            .Update(planeAnchor);
    }
}
}
```

The DidAddNode method fires when a new plane is detected in the scene (and corresponding ARPlaneAnchor is added to the scene). The DidUpdateNode method fires when ARKit's understanding of an existing detected plane changes. That is, the plane is larger than it originally thought, or the orientation is different. We can add our own custom code to either of these methods to do interesting things with this information.

## Plane Detection Example

An example ViewController class that detects planes and places a blue or red SCNPlane at the detected location depending on whether the plane is horizontal or vertical is shown in Listing 9-3.

*Listing 9-3.* A full end-to-end example of plane detection

```
public partial class ViewController : UIViewController
{
    private readonly ARSCNView sceneView;

    public ViewController(IntPtr handle) : base(handle)
    {
        this.sceneView = new ARSCNView
        {
            AutoenablesDefaultLighting = true,
            Delegate = new SceneViewDelegate()
        };

        this.View.AddSubview(this.sceneView);
    }
```

```csharp
        public override void ViewDidLoad()
        {
            base.ViewDidLoad();
            this.sceneView.Frame = this.View.Frame;
        }

        public override void ViewDidAppear(bool animated)
        {
            base.ViewDidAppear(animated);

            this.sceneView.Session.Run(new ARWorldTrackingConfiguration
            {
                PlaneDetection = ARPlaneDetection.Horizontal |
                ARPlaneDetection.Vertical,
                LightEstimationEnabled = true,
                WorldAlignment = ARWorldAlignment.GravityAndHeading
            }, ARSessionRunOptions.ResetTracking |
            ARSessionRunOptions.RemoveExistingAnchors);
        }

        public override void ViewDidDisappear(bool animated)
        {
            base.ViewDidDisappear(animated);
            this.sceneView.Session.Pause();
        }
    }

internal class PlaneNode : SCNNode
    {
        private readonly SCNPlane planeGeometry;

        public PlaneNode(ARPlaneAnchor planeAnchor, UIColor colour)
        {
            Geometry = (planeGeometry = CreateGeometry(planeAnchor,
            colour));
        }
```

```csharp
        public void Update(ARPlaneAnchor planeAnchor)
        {
            planeGeometry.Width = planeAnchor.Extent.X;
            planeGeometry.Height = planeAnchor.Extent.Z;

            Position = new SCNVector3(
                planeAnchor.Center.X,
                planeAnchor.Center.Y,
                planeAnchor.Center.Z);
        }

        private static SCNPlane CreateGeometry(ARPlaneAnchor planeAnchor,
        UIColor colour)
        {
            var material = new SCNMaterial();
            material.Diffuse.Contents = colour;
            material.DoubleSided = true;
            material.Transparency = 0.8f;

            var geometry = SCNPlane.Create(planeAnchor.Extent.X,
            planeAnchor.Extent.Z);
            geometry.Materials = new[] { material };

            return geometry;
        }
    }

public class SceneViewDelegate : ARSCNViewDelegate
    {
        private readonly IDictionary<NSUuid, PlaneNode> planeNodes = new
        Dictionary<NSUuid, PlaneNode>();

        public override void DidAddNode(
            ISCNSceneRenderer renderer, SCNNode node,
            ARAnchor anchor)
        {
            if (anchor is ARPlaneAnchor planeAnchor)
            {
                UIColor colour;
```

```
        if(planeAnchor.Alignment == ARPlaneAnchorAlignment.
        Vertical)
        {
            colour = UIColor.Red;
        }
        else {
            colour = UIColor.Blue;
        }

        var planeNode
            = new PlaneNode(planeAnchor, colour);
        var angle = (float)(-Math.PI / 2);
        planeNode.EulerAngles
            = new SCNVector3(angle, 0, 0);

        node.AddChildNode(planeNode);
        this.planeNodes.Add(anchor.Identifier, planeNode);
    }
}

public override void DidRemoveNode(
    ISCNSceneRenderer renderer, SCNNode node,
    ARAnchor anchor)
{
    if (anchor is ARPlaneAnchor planeAnchor)
    {
        this.planeNodes[anchor.Identifier]
            .RemoveFromParentNode();
        this.planeNodes.Remove(anchor.Identifier);
    }
}

public override void DidUpdateNode(
    ISCNSceneRenderer renderer, SCNNode node,
     ARAnchor anchor)
{
    if (anchor is ARPlaneAnchor planeAnchor)
```

```
        {
            this.planeNodes[anchor.Identifier]
                .Update(planeAnchor);
        }
    }
}
```

The result can be seen in Figure 9-1. Where the floor meets the wall, you can see how the materials of detected vertical and horizontal planes have been made red and blue, respectively. Opacity has been used so that you can still see the plane (wall or floor).

***Figure 9-1.***  *Differentiating between detected horizontal and vertical planes*

Of course, as discussed in Chapter 3, "Nodes, Geometries, Materials, and Anchors," as well as solid colors, geometry materials can also be images. By using a transparent PNG of a square and repeating/tiling the image on a detected plane, the following grid effect shown in Figure 9-2 can easily be achieved.

***Figure 9-2.*** *Grid image used on a detected plane*

# Turning Off Plane Detection

Plane detection can be CPU intensive; it is recommended that once you have identified the planes you desire, you turn off plane detection, as shown in Listing 9-4.

This is done by simply calling the .Run() method on the existing SceneView Session, this time with an ARWorldTrackingConfiguration with PlaneDetection set to ARPlaneDetection.None.

***Listing 9-4.*** It is recommended to turn off plane detection when no longer needed

```
...

// Turn off plane detection
var configuration = new ARWorldTrackingConfiguration
{
    PlaneDetection = ARPlaneDetection.None,
    LightEstimationEnabled = true,
};

this.sceneView.Session.Run(configuration, ARSessionRunOptions.None);

...
```

# Possible Applications

Plane detection is already used successfully by a number of businesses. Some major furniture retailers use it in their apps to detect the floor to allow users to place 3D models of their furniture in their living rooms. Some wallpaper and paint retailers use it to allow users of their apps to preview what a particular wallpaper or paint may look like on their walls.

Being able to detect planes in a scene also comes in useful if we want to have our virtual objects cast virtual shadows onto real surfaces as we saw in Chapter 7, "Lighting."

Like many aspects of AR, you need only use your imagination and you should hopefully be able to quickly identify many possible applications.

# Things to Try

Now that you know the theory of plane detection, you can try the following to use the feature in different ways.

**Identify detected vertical and horizontal planes and visually differentiate them.**
Set detected horizontal and vertical planes to a color of your choice, and play around with the opacity.

**Use a material with an image on detected planes.**
Rather than give your detected planes geometries a solid color, provide it with an image as its material. I have seen a (tiled) transparent grid image used to give detected planes an interesting look.

**Turn off plane detection.**
Practice turning off plane detection when you no longer need it. As mentioned, it is intensive and after you have detected your plane(s) sufficiently, often you do not need to detect more.

**Add touch interaction to your detected planes.**
Once you have read Chapter 12, "Touch Gestures and Interaction," come back and add touch gestures to your detected planes. Maybe change their color or some other aspect when tapped?

# Summary

Plane detection is an important concept to understand as it gives you the ability to do a number of interesting things like placing objects on detected surfaces.

Continuing on our theme of built-in detection abilities in ARKit, in the next chapter, we will look at image detection which allows us to identify predefined images in a scene and do some interesting things with them.

# CHAPTER 10

# Image Detection

Image detection is one of the most simple, fun, and useful abilities in Augmented Reality, and ARKit makes it super easy to do it.

In this chapter, we are going to see how we can use ARKit to recognize the location of predetermined images we want it to detect. Once we identify the location of a recognized image, we can do additional things such as replacing or adding to it. In this way, images are often used as markers to identify a location in 3D space.

## Adding Images as App Resources

One way of declaring the image(s) to detect is to package them along with the app. This is great if you know what image(s) you want to detect before you deploy the app.

© Lee Englestone 2021
L. Englestone, *.NET Developer's Guide to Augmented Reality in iOS,*
https://doi.org/10.1007/978-1-4842-6770-7_10

To do this:

1.  Double-click the `Assets.xcassets` folder in Solution Explorer to
    see the following screen shown in Figure 10-1.

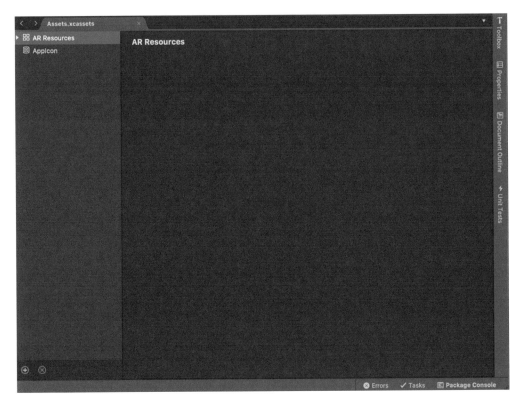

***Figure 10-1.***  *The Assets.xcassets folder*

2.  Click the bottom right green plus icon to bring up the "add"
    context menu and select "New AR Resource Group" to add a new
    AR Resource Group as shown in Figure 10-2.

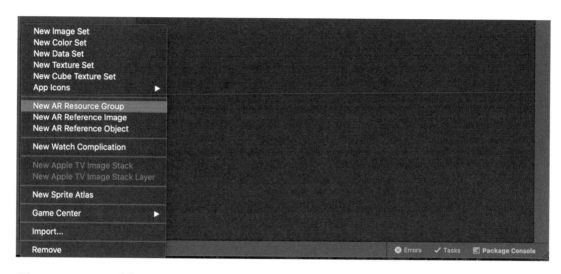

***Figure 10-2.*** *Add new AR Resource Group*

3. Right-click the new AR Resource Group and choose "New AR Reference Image" as shown in Figure 10-3.

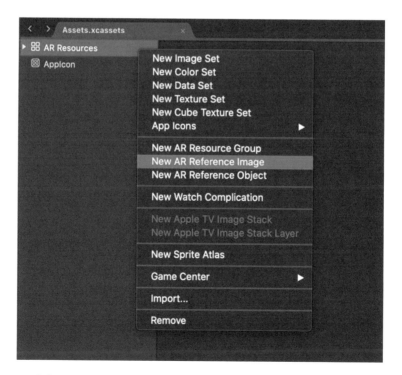

***Figure 10-3.*** *Add new AR Reference Image*

4.  Choose the image, provide its dimensions, and optionally
    rename it as shown in Figure 10-4.

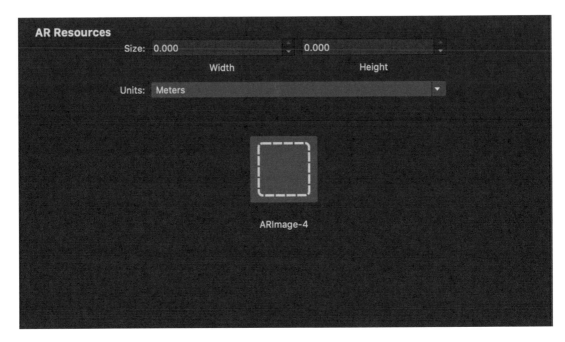

**Figure 10-4.** *Select Image and provide dimensions*

The dimensions you specify in Step 4 are the approximate dimensions the image will appear as in the real world. You specify these to help the app detect it.

# Detecting the Images

Now that we have added the images that we want to detect in the real world, we need to write the code to detect them and do something interesting when our app detects them.

As you can see in our constructor in Listing 10-1, we are telling our Scene View to use a Scene View Delegate. This class that can be seen in Listing 10-3 effectively handles the image detected event.

**Listing 10-1.** Setting a Scene View Delegate to use in the constructor

```
public ViewController(IntPtr handle) : base(handle)
{
    this.sceneView = new ARSCNView
    {
```

```
        AutoenablesDefaultLighting = true,
        Delegate = new SceneViewDelegate()
    };

    this.View.AddSubview(this.sceneView);
}
```

In Listing 10-2, we are retrieving the images that we previously added to the "AR Resources AR Reference Group" in Figure 10-4 and setting those as the images we want to detect.

***Listing 10-2.*** Declaring which images we wish to detect in the scene

```
public override void ViewDidAppear(bool animated)
{
    base.ViewDidAppear(animated);

    var detectionImages = ARReferenceImage.GetReferenceImagesInGroup("AR
Resources", null);

    this.sceneView.Session.Run(new ARWorldTrackingConfiguration
    {
        LightEstimationEnabled = true,
        WorldAlignment = ARWorldAlignment.GravityAndHeading,
        DetectionImages = detectionImages,
        MaximumNumberOfTrackedImages = 1

    });
}
```

In our SceneViewDelegate in Listing 10-3, we first check to see if the anchor that has been added to the scene is an `ARImageAnchor`. This will have been as a result of our app detecting the target image in the camera view. We can then get the corresponding name of the Reference Image that we provided in Figure 10-4 so we can identify *which* image has been detected.

Then next in this example, all we are doing are determining the dimensions of the detected image, creating a blue plane, and placing it at the location of the detected image, effectively covering the image.

It is worth noting that once you have placed virtual things on this node, if you change the orientation of the detected image in the real world, the orientation of your added plane will also be rotated.

This is a pretty cool effect and shows just how clever ARKit is; it is able to recognize that the orientation of the detected image is changing and can change the orientation of your virtual nodes accordingly in real time.

***Listing 10-3.*** Scene View Delegate handles image detection events

```
public class SceneViewDelegate : ARSCNViewDelegate
{
    public override void DidAddNode(
    ISCNSceneRenderer renderer, SCNNode node, ARAnchor anchor)
    {
        if (anchor is ARImageAnchor imageAnchor)
        {
            var detectedImage = imageAnchor.ReferenceImage;

            var width = detectedImage.PhysicalSize.Width;
            var length = detectedImage.PhysicalSize.Height;
            var planeNode = new PlaneNode(width, length, new SCNVector3(0,
            0, 0), UIColor.Blue);

            float angle = (float)(-Math.PI / 2);
            planeNode.EulerAngles
                = new SCNVector3(angle, 0, 0);

            node.AddChildNode(planeNode);
        }
    }
}
```

In Listing 10-4, we can see a simple class to encapsulate a plane node we used in Listing 10-3.

***Listing 10-4.*** Our custom PlaneNode

```
public class PlaneNode : SCNNode
{
    public PlaneNode(nfloat width, nfloat length,
        SCNVector3 position, UIColor colour)
    {
        var rootNode = new SCNNode
        {
            Geometry = CreateGeometry(width, length, colour),
            Position = position
        };

        AddChildNode(rootNode);
    }

    private static SCNGeometry CreateGeometry(
        nfloat width, nfloat length, UIColor colour)
    {
        var material = new SCNMaterial();
        material.Diffuse.Contents = colour;
        material.DoubleSided = false;

        var geometry = SCNPlane.Create(width, length);
        geometry.Materials = new[] { material };

        return geometry;
    }
}
```

# Dynamically Adding Images to Detect

As well as packaging the image(s) which you want to detect along with the app, it is also possible to dynamically add images to detect at runtime. This is especially useful if you don't know which images you need to detect at compile time.

For example, you could make a call to the Amazon API, return the images for the top-selling book front covers, and add those to the app to detect. Then provide further functionality when those book covers are detected such as retrieving and displaying review information in AR next to the detected book.

# Things to Try

Now that you know how to detect expected images in a scene, you may wish to try and see what you can do with that functionality. Here are some ideas.

**Replace the detected image with another image.**

When you have detected the image, try placing another image on top of the detected image (apparently replacing it).

**Replace the detected image with a video.**

After you have detected the image, place a video at the location of the detected image and play it. See Chapter 8, "Video and Sound," for how to add a video to your scene.

**Place a 3D model at the location of the detected image.**

After detecting the image, place a 3D model at the location of the detected image. See Chapter 13, "3D Models," for how to add a 3D model to your scene.

*Figure 10-5.* *Placing a 3D model on a detected image*

Image detection can be used to create some interesting effects as can be seen in Figure 10-5 which shows a 3D model placed on top of the detected image and Figure 10-6 which shows floating images added on top of a detected image.

***Figure 10-6.*** *Adding floating images to a detected image*

## Summary

Image detection is a very useful feature in Augmented Reality often used by marketers to add AR experiences to their products.

Another amazing feature that comes right out of the box with ARKit is the ability to not only track faces but also facial expressions. We will explore this in the next chapter, "Face Tracking and Expression Detection."

# CHAPTER 11

# Face Tracking and Expression Detection

Just in case you thought that the built-in Augmented Reality functionality that ARKit has to offer wasn't amazing enough, you won't believe what you can do with face tracking and facial expression detection. By using the front-facing camera, it can track multiple faces and even the expressions on them.

## Tracking Faces

Out of the box ARKit gives us the ability to track up to three different faces in a scene. To be clear, that means detecting faces and following them around the scene.

Please note that without additional coding, ARKit cannot recognize *who* the faces belong to. ARKit can only *detect* that there *are* faces in front of the camera, not *who* they belong to.

L. Englestone, *.NET Developer's Guide to Augmented Reality in iOS*,
https://doi.org/10.1007/978-1-4842-6770-7_11

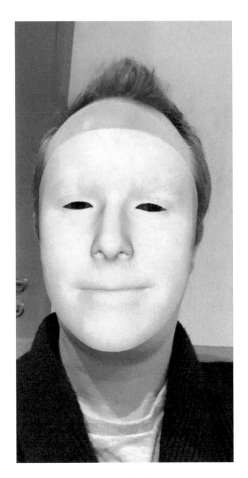

*Figure 11-1.* *Up to three faces can be tracked in a scene and their geometry retrieved and manipulated*

It is worth noting that older iOS devices may not support face tracking. It is recommended that you check the ARFaceTrackingConfiguration.IsSupported property before trying to call the face tracking functionality as if your device does not support it, the app will just crash and exit if it attempts to call the functionality. If face tracking is not supported, you may wish to show a message to the user telling them this.

In Listing 11-1, we are running our Session, this time with an ARFaceTrackingConfiguration which by default uses the front camera on the phone and allows us to track faces in the scene as demonstrated in Figure 11-1.

We are then using a Scene View Delegate to handle the events that are fired when a face is detected, moves, or changes. More specifically, in the following code example, when a new face is detected in the scene (which places an ARFaceAnchor at the relevant position), we are retrieving the facial geometry and setting it to be the geometry of the node that is placed at the location of the ARFaceAnchor and setting it to be 80% opaque.

***Listing 11-1.*** Tracking people's faces in the scene

```
public partial class ViewController : UIViewController
{
    private readonly ARSCNView sceneView;

    public ViewController(IntPtr handle) : base(handle)
    {
        this.sceneView = new ARSCNView
        {
            AutoenablesDefaultLighting = true,
            Delegate = new SceneViewDelegate()
        };

        this.View.AddSubview(this.sceneView);
    }

    public override void ViewDidLoad()
    {
        base.ViewDidLoad();
        this.sceneView.Frame = this.View.Frame;
    }

    public override void ViewDidAppear(bool animated)
    {
        base.ViewDidAppear(animated);

        var faceTrackingConfiguration = new ARFaceTrackingConfiguration()
        {
            LightEstimationEnabled = true,
            MaximumNumberOfTrackedFaces = 1
        };

        this.sceneView.Session.Run(faceTrackingConfiguration);
    }
```

```csharp
    public override void ViewDidDisappear(bool animated)
    {
        base.ViewDidDisappear(animated);
        this.sceneView.Session.Pause();
    }
}

public class SceneViewDelegate : ARSCNViewDelegate
{
    public override void DidAddNode(ISCNSceneRenderer renderer, SCNNode
    node, ARAnchor anchor)
    {
        if (anchor is ARFaceAnchor faceAnchor)
        {
            var faceGeometry = ARSCNFaceGeometry.Create(renderer.
            GetDevice());

            node.Geometry = faceGeometry;
            node.Opacity = 0.8f;
        }
    }

    public override void DidUpdateNode(ISCNSceneRenderer renderer, SCNNode
    node, ARAnchor anchor)
    {
        if (anchor is ARFaceAnchor)
        {
            var faceAnchor = anchor as ARFaceAnchor;
            var faceGeometry = node.Geometry as ARSCNFaceGeometry;
            faceGeometry.Update(faceAnchor.Geometry);
        }
    }
}
```

Instead of using a plane solid color for the facial geometry, if we wanted, we could use an image instead. So we could place an image on top of someone's face, making them look like a masked superhero, for example.

It is easy to doubt the usefulness of the real-world applications of this functionality and just think of it as a bit of fun; however, there are successful businesses that have implemented this type of facial tracking to great effect. For example, being able to track the orientation of faces, some businesses show what different glasses look like when worn by the user by adding 3D models of different styles of glasses onto the user's facial geometry. Impressive stuff.

# Recognize Facial Expressions

As well as tracking the presence of faces in our scene, we are also able to detect a surprisingly large number of different facial expressions on those faces (in fact, over 50 different facial expressions).

In Figure 11-2, I am using `material.FillMode = SCNFillMode.Lines` that we first mentioned in Chapter 3, "Nodes, Geometries, Materials, and Anchors," with a default color of white and then, when detecting a *mouth funnel*, changing the line color to yellow.

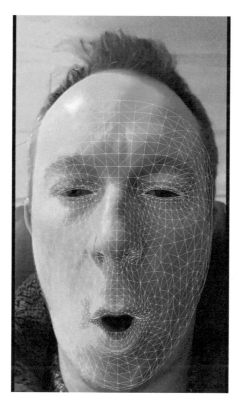

***Figure 11-2.*** *More than 50 different facial expressions can be detected*

Using `SCNFillMode.Lines`, we can really see how ARKit can detect the contours of the face. It's no surprise that it can infer a number of facial expressions.

Here is a complete list of detectable facial expressions (I told you there were a lot):

- eyeBlinkLeft, eyeBlinkRight
- eyeLookDownLeft, eyeLookDownRight
- eyeLookInLeft, eyeLookInRight
- eyeLookOutLeft, eyeLookOutRight
- eyeLookUpLeft, eyeLookUpRight
- eyeSquintLeft, eyeSquintRight
- eyeWideLeft, eyeWideRight
- jawForward
- jawLeft, jawRight
- jawOpen
- mouthClose
- mouthFunnel
- mouthPucker
- mouthLeft, mouthRight
- mouthSmileLeft, mouthSmileRight
- mouthFrownLeft, mouthFrownRight
- mouthDimpleLeft, mouthDimpleRight
- mouthStretchLeft, mouthStretchRight
- mouthRollLower, mouthRollUpper
- mouthShrugLower, mouthShrugUpper
- mouthPressLeft, mouthPressRight
- mouthLowerDownLeft, mouthLowerDownRight
- mouthUpperUpLeft, mouthUpperUpRight

- browDownLeft, browDownRight

- browInnerUp

- browOuterUpLeft

- browOuterUpRight

- cheekPuff

- cheekSquintLeft, cheekSquintRight

- noseSneerLeft, noseSneerRight

- tongueOut

The description of each expression can be found here in Apple's official documentation: https://developer.apple.com/documentation/arkit/arfaceanchor/ blendshapelocation.

ARKit even allows us to track multiple expressions simultaneously (e.g., right eye closed and tongue out) as well as tracking the relative presence of those expressions. For example, each expression has a floating value between 0 and 1 to denote the complete absence of the expression or the complete presence of it, that is, to track whether the tongue is not out at all, a little bit, or completely.

Listing 11-2 shows how we can set up and use ARFaceTrackingConfiguration when we start our session.

***Listing 11-2.*** Recognizing a few of the facial expressions

```
public partial class ViewController : UIViewController
{
    private readonly ARSCNView sceneView;

    public ViewController(IntPtr handle) : base(handle)
    {
        this.sceneView = new ARSCNView
        {
            AutoenablesDefaultLighting = true,
            Delegate = new SceneViewDelegate()
        };
```

```csharp
        this.View.AddSubview(this.sceneView);
    }

    public override void ViewDidLoad()
    {
        base.ViewDidLoad();
        this.sceneView.Frame = this.View.Frame;
    }

    public override void ViewDidAppear(bool animated)
    {
        base.ViewDidAppear(animated);

        var faceTrackingConfiguration = new
            ARFaceTrackingConfiguration()
        {
            LightEstimationEnabled = true,
            MaximumNumberOfTrackedFaces = 1
        };

        this.sceneView.Session.Run(faceTrackingConfiguration);
    }

    public override void ViewDidDisappear(bool animated)
    {
        base.ViewDidDisappear(animated);
        this.sceneView.Session.Pause();
    }
}

public class SceneViewDelegate : ARSCNViewDelegate
{
    public override void DidAddNode(ISCNSceneRenderer renderer, SCNNode
    node, ARAnchor anchor)
    {
        if (anchor is ARFaceAnchor)
        {
```

```
    var faceGeometry = ARSCNFaceGeometry.Create(renderer.
    GetDevice());
    node.Geometry = faceGeometry;
    node.Geometry.FirstMaterial.FillMode =
        SCNFillMode.Lines;
    }
}

public override void DidUpdateNode(ISCNSceneRenderer renderer, SCNNode
node, ARAnchor anchor)
{
    if (anchor is ARFaceAnchor)
    {
        var faceAnchor = anchor as ARFaceAnchor;
        var faceGeometry = node.Geometry as
            ARSCNFaceGeometry;
        var expressionThreshold = 0.5f;

        faceGeometry.Update(faceAnchor.Geometry);

        if (faceAnchor.BlendShapes.EyeBlinkLeft > expressionThreshold
            || faceAnchor.BlendShapes.EyeBlinkRight >
                expressionThreshold)
        {
            ChangeFaceColour(node, UIColor.Blue);
            return;
        }

        if (faceAnchor.BlendShapes.MouthSmileLeft > expressionThreshold
            || faceAnchor.BlendShapes.MouthSmileRight >
                expressionThreshold)
        {
            ChangeFaceColour(node, UIColor.SystemPinkColor);
            return;
        }
```

```
        if (faceAnchor.BlendShapes.EyeLookOutLeft > expressionThreshold
            || faceAnchor.BlendShapes.EyeLookOutRight >
                expressionThreshold)
        {
            ChangeFaceColour(node, UIColor.Magenta);
            return;
        }

        if (faceAnchor.BlendShapes.TongueOut > expressionThreshold)
        {
            ChangeFaceColour(node, UIColor.Red);
            return;
        }

        if (faceAnchor.BlendShapes.CheekPuff > expressionThreshold)
        {
            ChangeFaceColour(node, UIColor.Orange);
            return;
        }

        ChangeFaceColour(node, UIColor.White);
    }
}

private void ChangeFaceColour(SCNNode faceGeometry, UIColor colour)
{
    var material = new SCNMaterial();
    material.Diffuse.Contents = colour;
    material.FillMode = SCNFillMode.Lines;

    faceGeometry.Geometry.FirstMaterial = material;
}
}
```

Notice in Listing 11-2 we are using SCNFillMode.Lines as the materials FillMode to better show the contours of the facial geometry.

# Things to Try

**Add new nodes and shapes to your detected face.**

Create and add additional nodes (e.g., shapes or images) to the node containing the facial mesh in the DidUpdateNode method – for example, placing a basic "hat" on someone's head, giving them a beard or moustache, or showing an image (on a 2D plane) containing information on that person.

**Treat different tracked faces differently.**

As mentioned, ARKit can track up to three faces simultaneously. Try assigning a different color to each face being tracked.

**Use an image for the face material.**

Instead of a solid color for the detected face node material, try using an image for the material. With the right image, you could make the user's face look like a Spider-Man mask or similar. Use your imagination!

# Summary

Face tracking and facial expression detection allows us to make augmented personal by involving the user's face in the experiences. The use cases of this can range from a bit of fun to previewing wearable products, a very popular use case for Augmented Reality apps.

So far in the book, we have looked at placing items in our scene; in the next chapter, we will look at how we can interact with those objects as we learn about touch gestures and interaction.

# CHAPTER 12

# Touch Gestures and Interaction

So far, we've looked at different ways of adding virtual objects to our Augmented Reality scenes. Wouldn't it be great if you could interact with them too? Oh, wait. You can, and that is what we will look at in this chapter.

## Gesture Recognizers

There are a number of predefined ways of touching your device's screen that can be automatically translated into what are called gestures and fire an equivalent `UIGestureRecognizer`. Then based on the type of gesture made, if any of the virtual items in your scene are touched, they can be manipulated accordingly.

We are able to recognize a number of different gestures on the device's screen, and in this chapter, we will look at how we can react to them.

- Tap
- Rotate
- Pinch
- Swipe
- Long press

We will also look at how we can alter the default behaviors of these gestures and extend them. For example, easily changing the tap gesture into a double-tap gesture or changing how long a press is required for a long press gesture.

© Lee Englestone 2021
L. Englestone, *.NET Developer's Guide to Augmented Reality in iOS*,
https://doi.org/10.1007/978-1-4842-6770-7_12

You must bear in mind that device screens are two-dimensional and therefore our gestures are in 2D, so it is sometimes necessary to define in the code which axis you are wanting to manipulate your virtual item in. For example, when using the panning gesture up or down or left or right, it makes sense to move an object along the Y and X axes in 3D space, but how do you enable the user to move something along the Z axis to be closer or further? You may wish to use multiple gesture recognizers to achieve your desired experience.

# Hooking Up Gesture Recognizers

In order for our app to respond to different types of touch, we need to tell our SceneView to listen for the gestures that we want it to recognize as can be seen in Listing 12-1.

Then in the subsequent listings in this chapter, we can look at example code that runs for those types of gestures.

***Listing 12-1.*** We can tell our app to respond to a number of different gestures

```
public override void ViewDidAppear(bool animated)
{
    base.ViewDidAppear(animated);

    ...

    var panGesture = new UIPanGestureRecognizer(HandlePanGesture);
    this.sceneView.AddGestureRecognizer(panGesture);

    var rotateGesture = new UIRotationGestureRecognizer
    (HandleRotateGesture);
    this.sceneView.AddGestureRecognizer(rotateGesture);

    var pinchGesture = new UIPinchGestureRecognizer(HandlePinchGesture);
    this.sceneView.AddGestureRecognizer(pinchGesture);

    var tapGesture = new UITapGestureRecognizer(HandleTapGesture);
    this.sceneView.AddGestureRecognizer(tapGesture);

    var swipeGesture = new UISwipeGestureRecognizer(HandleSwipeGesture);
    this.sceneView.AddGestureRecognizer(swipeGesture);
```

```
    var longPressGesture = new UILongPressGestureRecognizer(HandleLongPress
    Gesture);
    this.sceneView.AddGestureRecognizer(longPressGesture);

    ...
}
```

# Tapping

We can detect whether a tap on the screen touches a virtual object in our scene and react accordingly. We can also insist on a minimum number of taps if we wanted, for example, to make it a double-click gesture recognizer. In Listing 12-2, when a node is tapped, we are changing its color to be black.

***Listing 12-2.*** Tap UIGestureRecognizer

```
private void HandleTapGesture(UITapGestureRecognizer sender)
{
    var areaTapped = sender.View as SCNView;
    var location = sender.LocationInView(areaTapped);
    var hitTestResults = areaTapped.HitTest(
        location, new SCNHitTestOptions());

    var hitTest = hitTestResults.FirstOrDefault();

    if (hitTest == null)
        return;

    var node = hitTest.Node;

    var material = new SCNMaterial();
    material.Diffuse.Contents = UIColor.Black;
    node.Geometry.FirstMaterial = material;
}
```

If you are using the tap gesture to "select" a virtual object in your scene, you may want to do other things to denote that it is "selected," such as change its color or scale, for example, something to help denote that the object that has been tapped has focus and you want your user to know what has been tapped/selected.

# Pinching

By placing two fingers on the screen and pinching them together or un-pinching them apart, we can scale the virtual item you are pinching larger or smaller. This can be achieved using the code shown in Listing 12-3.

---

**Note**   When handling the Pinch Gesture and scaling nodes as shown in Listing 12-2, it is necessary to reset the sender scale to 1 to avoid unusual behavior.

---

*Listing 12-3.* Pinch UIGestureRecognizer

```
private void HandlePinchGesture(UIPinchGestureRecognizer sender)
{
    var areaPinched = sender.View as SCNView;
    var location = sender.LocationInView(areaPinched);
    var hitTestResults = areaPinched.HitTest(
        location, new SCNHitTestOptions());

    var hitTest = hitTestResults.FirstOrDefault();

    if (hitTest == null)
        return;

    var node = hitTest.Node;

    var scaleX = (float)sender.Scale * node.Scale.X;
    var scaleY = (float)sender.Scale * node.Scale.Y;
    var scaleZ = (float)sender.Scale * node.Scale.Z;

    node.Scale = new SCNVector3(scaleX, scaleY, scaleZ);
    sender.Scale = 1;
}
```

Pinching is a great way to scale items in your scene. It is often used to scale items or zoom in/out in other popular apps so it will feel natural to a user to use pinching in this way.

# Rotating

By placing two fingers on the screen atop a virtual object and rotating their position clockwise or counterclockwise, we can rotate the virtual item in a given axis.

In Listing 12-4, we are rotating the orientation of the touched object in the Z axis when we detect this gesture.

***Listing 12-4.*** Rotate UIGestureRecognizer

```
private void HandleRotateGesture(UIRotationGestureRecognizer sender)
{
    var areaTouched = sender.View as SCNView;
    var location = sender.LocationInView(areaTouched);
    var hitTestResults = areaTouched.HitTest(
        location, new SCNHitTestOptions());

    var hitTest = hitTestResults.FirstOrDefault();

    if (hitTest == null)
        return;

    var node = hitTest.Node;

    newAngleZ = (float)(-sender.Rotation);
    newAngleZ += currentAngleZ;
    node.EulerAngles = new SCNVector3(node.EulerAngles.X,
        node.EulerAngles.Y, newAngleZ);
}
```

You may need to try translating the rotate gesture to change the orientation of the object in different axis to achieve the correct result.

# Panning

By placing your finger on the screen atop a virtual object and dragging it across the screen in any direction, then releasing, we can move an item from its original position to a new one along a given axis. Listing 12-5 shows how you could respond to a pan gesture.

***Listing 12-5.*** Pan UIGestureRecognizer

```
private void HandlePanGesture(UIPanGestureRecognizer sender)
{
    var areaPanned = sender.View as SCNView;
    var location = sender.LocationInView(areaPanned);
    var hitTestResults = areaPanned.HitTest(location,
        new SCNHitTestOptions());

    var hitTest = hitTestResults.FirstOrDefault();

    if (hitTest == null)
        return;

    var node = hitTest.Node;

    if (sender.State == UIGestureRecognizerState.Changed)
    {
        var translate = sender.TranslationInView(areaPanned);

        // Only allow movement vertically or horizontally
        // High values are used so that the movement is smooth
        node.LocalTranslate(
            new SCNVector3((float)translate.X / 10000f,
                (float)-translate.Y / 10000, 0.0f));
    }
}
```

As mentioned in the introduction, we can only interact with our device screens in two dimensions using touch gestures (vertically and horizontally), so when a pan gesture is recognized, we need to choose which of the two axes we want to move the object in.

Whether you are looking at an object from the side or from above may determine which axis you wish to move them along.

# Swiping

By placing your finger on the screen atop a virtual object and swiping it across the screen either vertically or horizontally, we can have our virtual objects respond to swipes. In Listing 12-6, when a swiping gesture is detected on a node, it will turn it pink.

***Listing 12-6.*** Swipe UIGestureRecognizer

```
private void HandleSwipeGesture(UISwipeGestureRecognizer sender)
{
    var areaSwiped = sender.View as SCNView;
    var location = sender.LocationInView(areaSwiped);
    var hitTestResults = areaSwiped.HitTest(
        location, new SCNHitTestOptions());

    var hitTest = hitTestResults.FirstOrDefault();

    if (hitTest == null)
        return;

    var node = hitTest.Node;

    var material = new SCNMaterial();
    material.Diffuse.Contents = UIColor.SystemPinkColor;
    node.Geometry.FirstMaterial = material;
}
```

The swiping gesture is similar to a fast pan gesture and is often used to remove or dismiss things in other apps, so you could do the same with your app if you wished.

# Long Press

By placing your finger on the screen atop a virtual object and holding it there, we can have our virtual object respond to the long press gesture. In Listing 12-7, when a long press gesture is detected on a node, it will turn it orange.

***Listing 12-7.*** Long Press UIGestureRecognizer

```
private void HandleLongPressGesture(UILongPressGestureRecognizer sender)
{
    var areaPressed = sender.View as SCNView;
    var location = sender.LocationInView(areaPressed);
    var hitTestResults = areaPressed.HitTest(
        location, new SCNHitTestOptions());

    var hitTest = hitTestResults.FirstOrDefault();

    if (hitTest == null)
        return;

    var node = hitTest.Node;

    var material = new SCNMaterial();
    material.Diffuse.Contents = UIColor.Orange;
    node.Geometry.FirstMaterial = material;
}
```

You could use a long press as a type of "special selection" and as a way to differentiate from just a simple "tap" gesture.

It is possible to change the `MinimumPressDuration`, which is the number of seconds which the press needs to happen for to be considered a long press and fire which by default is 0.5.

# Things to Try

Touch interactions are some of the more tactile interactions that we have with our Augmented Reality experiences. You can fine-tune them to suit your needs.

**Add touch gesture recognizers to your app.**

Try adding tap, rotate, pan, swipe, and long press touch gesture recognizers to your app and have them manipulate objects in your scene in different ways.

**Alter the MinimumPressDuration of the long press gesture.**

Try changing the `MinimumPressDuration` required to fire a long press gesture from the default 0.5 seconds to 2 seconds.

**Change the minimum number of fingers required in the gestures.**

Try enforcing two or more fingers be involved in the gesture before it is fired using the `NumberOfTouchesRequired` property. By default, it is 1.

**Require a double-tap condition to activate a tap gesture.**

You can change the `NumberOfTapsRequired` property on the tap gesture recognizer to 2, to change a tap gesture recognizer into a double-tap recognizer. You don't need much imagination to figure out how to implement a triple-tap gesture recognizer.

# Summary

You should now know how to interact with any item you place into your AR experiences in several different ways including moving them around in 3D space. The trick is to make your interactions intuitive and behave in a manner your user would expect.

So far, we have been placing simple shapes and images into our scene; in the next chapter, we will look at how we can place much more interesting objects into our scene, 3D models.

# CHAPTER 13

# 3D Models

In this chapter, we will look at how we can take existing 3D models and use them in your Augmented Reality scenes as well as discuss the popular free 3D tool "Blender" and how it can be used to create your own 3D models.

We've already seen that SceneKit allows us to use seven or eight different primitive 3D models such as boxes, spheres, cylinders, planes, and so on, but they are rather limited and unexciting. By using existing 3D models or even creating our own, we can make our Augmented Reality experiences more impressive and engaging.

## Importing 3D Models

Fortunately, it is easy to import existing 3D models into a scene and SceneKit/ARKit support several 3D file formats.

The following 3D model formats can be used in our scenes:

- .dae
- .usdz
- .usda
- .usd and .usdc
- .rcproject and .reality
- .obj and .mtl
- .abc
- .ply
- .stl
- .scn

© Lee Englestone 2021
L. Englestone, *.NET Developer's Guide to Augmented Reality in iOS*,
https://doi.org/10.1007/978-1-4842-6770-7_13

There are an increasing number of websites and creators specializing in pre-made 3D models. I have found free3d.com to be an excellent place to find free and cheap pre-made 3D models.

In Listing 13-1, we can see how simple it is to import a 3D model into our scene.

It is worth noting that once the 3D model has been added to the scene as a SCNNode, it is just like any other SCNNode, so we can change its position, scale, orientation, materials, and so on. In fact, sometimes imported 3D models are far too big for our scene, so we need to change the scale of the nodes before they will fit into our scene.

And of course you can combine other effects we covered in previous chapters with your 3D model. For example, you could use animations to have the 3D model slowly spin or set its opacity to have it slightly transparent or have it fade into the scene.

One thing you must bear in mind when retrieving the 3D model from the file is that you will need to retrieve the specific node you wish to retrieve from the file by name as can be seen in Listing 13-1. Fortunately, Xcode can be quite useful in determining the name of the node you wish to add, as can be seen in Figure 13-1.

***Listing 13-1.*** Adding a 3D model to a scene

```
public override void ViewDidAppear(bool animated)
{
    base.ViewDidAppear(animated);

    this.sceneView.Session.Run(
        new ARWorldTrackingConfiguration());

    SCNScene sceneFromFile = SCNScene.FromFile(
        "art.scnassets/tree.dae");

    SCNNode model = sceneFromFile.RootNode.FindChildNode(
        childName:"SomeChildName", recursively: true);

    // How to scale or position the node model if needed
    model.Scale = new SCNVector3(0.2f, 0.2f, 0.2f);
    model.Position = new SCNVector3(0, -0.2f, 0);

    this.sceneView.Scene.RootNode.AddChildNode(model);
}
```

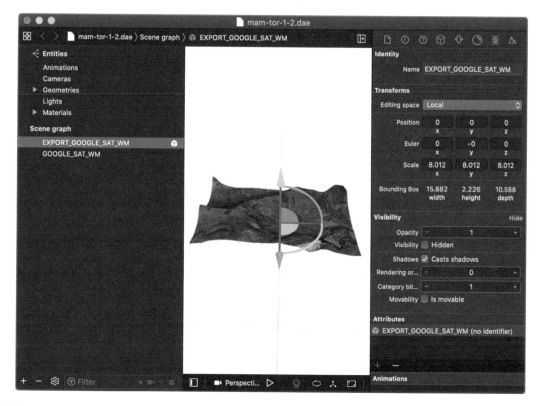

**Figure 13-1.**  *Xcode is useful for finding the name of your root node if you do not know it*

To reiterate, if you have possession of the 3D model file but don't know the name of the root node, then if you open the file in Xcode, you should be able to click around parts of the model and navigate the scene graph to find the root node name.

# Creating Your Own 3D Models in Blender

If you want to create your own 3D models in your Augmented Reality experiences, I strongly recommend you consider learning how to use a 3D modelling tool called Blender. It is something that I am slowly learning myself.

For starters, it is a free tool that is not only powerful but at the same time accessible to beginners willing to put in the time to learn it, and is becoming increasingly popular. In fact, many film studios have started using Blender for creating 3D models and effects rather than using expensive industry standard alternatives. There are also a lot of tutorials online about how to create various 3D models ranging from doughnuts to furniture to castles and cars.

For example, as can be seen in Figure 13-2, using Blender and a plug-in called "BlenderGIS," we can produce a 3D model of any terrain returned from Google Maps, then export it and use it in our AR experiences.

***Figure 13-2.*** *Using 3D models from Blender in our AR experiences can be very impressive*

You can see in Figure 13-2, this example is also using shadows (from Chapter 7, "Lighting") to help the user to understand how high off the ground it is floating and make it look more real.

---

**Note**    Whether you create, export, and import your own 3D model or obtain and use a pre-made 3D model, if that model comes with textures (usually one or more image files), you will need to make sure you package those along with your 3D model. Often the 3D model file will reference the image texture files locations relatively, so they often need to be stored in the same folder or at least relative to where the 3D model file resides.

---

# Add Shadows, Animations, and Make Interactive

By this point, we have already covered a few other concepts that we can use in conjunction with our 3D models. We can add lighting and shadows to make the 3D models look more real. We can use animations to make the 3D models more dynamic.

# Things to Try

You could spend all day playing around with 3D models in your Augmented Reality scenes; however, here are a few ideas of things you could try.

**Add a pre-made 3D model to your app.**

Obtain a supported, 3D model file, add it to your project, and place it in your scene.

**Create a simple model in Blender and use it in your app.**

Create a basic model in Blender; it doesn't have to be complicated. Then export it into a supported file type, add it to your project, then use it in your scene.

**Use touch gestures to interact with 3D models in your scene.**

Get your 3D model to respond to the touch interactions discussed in Chapter 12, "Touch Gestures and Interaction."

**Add animations to your 3D model.**

Use some of the animations (actions) discussed in Chapter 5, "Animations," to animate the scale, position, or opacity of a 3D model in your scene.

**Use 3D models with Image detection.**

Try adding a 3D model to an image detected in a scene. You'll notice that if you rotate the orientation of the detected image, the orientation of the 3D model will change similarly.

# Summary

As well as basic 3D shapes, which we learned about previously, you should now be aware of how more complex 3D models can be added to and used in your AR experiences. You can either obtain pre-made ones or even build and use your own using a 3D modelling tool like Blender.

With various models and shapes in our scene now, we should look at ways that we can allow them to simulate interaction with each other and their physical environment through the use of simulated physics. If you are thinking this sounds complicated, don't worry. ARKit has some built-in physics abilities so that we don't have to worry about the maths and complexities as we shall see in the next chapter, "Physics."

# CHAPTER 14

# Physics

Another amazing thing that SceneKit provides us with right out of the box that we can use in our Augmented Reality experiences is a physics engine. This means that we can give the items we place in our scenes the ability to interact with each other as you would expect if they were real objects.

We can do this by setting the SCNNode.PhysicsBody property on our SCNNodes.

## Giving an Item a Rigid Structure

We can give our nodes some virtual substance beyond a visual appearance so that things can collide with it as if it were solid as shown in Listing 14-1.

We set our nodes' physics body to be solid by calling PhysicsBody = SCNPhysicsBody.CreateKinematicBody().

***Listing 14-1.*** Making a 2D plane rigid

```
var material = new SCNMaterial();
material.Diffuse.Contents = UIColor.DarkGray;

var geometry = SCNPlane.Create(width, length);
geometry.Materials = new[] { material };

var planeNode = new SCNNode
{
    Geometry = geometry,
    PhysicsBody = SCNPhysicsBody.CreateKinematicBody(),
    EulerAngles = new SCNVector3((float)(-Math.PI / 2), 0, 0)
};
```

© Lee Englestone 2021
L. Englestone, *.NET Developer's Guide to Augmented Reality in iOS,*
https://doi.org/10.1007/978-1-4842-6770-7_14

Once we have done this, other nodes with a PhysicsBody will collide with it if they try to occupy the same space, and more importantly, we can place items on top of this solid plane.

# Applying Gravity to an Object

Instead of placing items in our scene at a particular position and having them effectively "float" there remaining in that position, we can tell items to mimic being effected by gravity, that is, be pulled straight down until they are stopped by hitting another virtual item that has been given a rigid body as we did previously in Figure 14-1.

To have a SCNNode be pulled down like gravity, we can set its `PhysicsBody` to be a Dynamic Body `PhysicsBody = SCNPhysicsBody.CreateDynamicBody()` as shown in Listing 14-2.

If you do use gravity in your scene and on your nodes, I suggest you also use a Kinematic Body as a type of physical surface or floor; otherwise, you'll find your nodes just fall off the screen toward the center of the earth! In fact, they will keep falling while they are well out of view (but will still use app memory!).

By placing a kinetic plane underneath, we can stop that unusual and undesired behavior and mimic something more like a real-world experiences.

***Listing 14-2.*** Making a cube effected by gravity

```
var material = new SCNMaterial();
material.Diffuse.Contents = UIColor.Green;

var size = 0.05f;
var geometry = SCNBox.Create(size, size, size, 0);
geometry.Materials = new[] { material };

var cubeNode = new SCNNode
{
    Geometry = geometry,
    PhysicsBody = SCNPhysicsBody.CreateDynamicBody(),
};
```

# Combining Gravity and Solid Objects

In the following example (Listing 14-3), we are placing a 2D plane in the scene and giving it a solid rigid physical attribute. We are then spawning cubes above the 2D plane that are affected by gravity and are pulled downward until they hit and come to rest on the solid 2D plane.

*Listing 14-3.* Using gravity to drop solid cubes onto a solid 2D plane

```
public partial class ViewController : UIViewController
    {
        private readonly ARSCNView sceneView;

        public ViewController(IntPtr handle) : base(handle)
        {
            this.sceneView = new ARSCNView();
            this.View.AddSubview(this.sceneView);
        }

        public override void ViewDidLoad()
        {
            base.ViewDidLoad();
            this.sceneView.Frame = this.View.Frame;
        }

        public override void ViewDidAppear(bool animated)
        {
            base.ViewDidAppear(animated);

            this.sceneView.Session.Run(new ARWorldTrackingConfiguration
            {
                LightEstimationEnabled = true,
                WorldAlignment = ARWorldAlignment.Gravity
            });

            var planeNode = new PlaneNode(width:0.5f, length:0.5f, UIColor.
            DarkGray);
```

```
        this.sceneView.Scene.RootNode.AddChildNode(planeNode);
}

public override void TouchesEnded(NSSet touches, UIEvent evt)
{
    base.TouchesEnded(touches, evt);

    if (!(touches.AnyObject is UITouch touch))
        return;

    var point = touch.LocationInView(this.sceneView);
    var hits = this.sceneView.HitTest(point, new
    SCNHitTestOptions());
    var hit = hits.FirstOrDefault();

    if (hit == null)
        return;

    var node = hit.Node;

    if (node == null)
        return;

    var cubeNode = new CubeNode(0.05f, UIColor.Green)
    {
        Position = new SCNVector3(
            hit.WorldCoordinates.X,
            hit.WorldCoordinates.Y + 0.1f,
            hit.WorldCoordinates.Z
        )
    };

    this.sceneView.Scene.RootNode.AddChildNode(cubeNode);
}

public override void ViewDidDisappear(bool animated)
{
    base.ViewDidDisappear(animated);
    this.sceneView.Session.Pause();
}
```

```
    public override void DidReceiveMemoryWarning()
    {
        base.DidReceiveMemoryWarning();
    }
}

public class PlaneNode : SCNNode
{
    public PlaneNode(float width, float length, UIColor color)
    {
        Geometry = CreateGeometry(width, length, color);
        PhysicsBody = SCNPhysicsBody.CreateKinematicBody();
        EulerAngles = new SCNVector3((float)(-Math.PI / 2), 0, 0);
    }

    private static SCNGeometry CreateGeometry(float width, float
    length, UIColor color)
    {
        var material = new SCNMaterial();
        material.Diffuse.Contents = color;
        material.DoubleSided = true;

        var geometry = SCNPlane.Create(width, length);
        geometry.Materials = new[] { material };
        return geometry;
    }
}

public class CubeNode : SCNNode
{
    public CubeNode(float size, UIColor color)
    {
        Geometry = CreateGeometry(size, color);
        Position = new SCNVector3(0, size / 2, 0);
        PhysicsBody = SCNPhysicsBody.CreateDynamicBody();
    }
```

```
private static SCNGeometry CreateGeometry(float size, UIColor
color)
{
    var material = new SCNMaterial();
    material.Diffuse.Contents = color;

    var geometry = SCNBox.Create(size, size, size, 0);
    geometry.Materials = new[] { material };
    return geometry;
}
}
```

***Figure 14-1.*** *Dropping solid cubes onto a solid plane*

# Applying Force

As well as applying basic physics to our nodes like gravity, giving them a solid structure, and allowing them to touch each other, we can also apply a force to them.

In Listing 14-4, we place a single box on a plane and, when touching the box node, apply a large force to it propelling forward and off the plane. You can play around with the amount of force to apply and see how the node is affected when touched.

*Listing 14-4.* Apply force to an object in Augmented Reality

```
public partial class ViewController : UIViewController
    {
        private readonly ARSCNView sceneView;

        public ViewController(IntPtr handle) : base(handle)
        {
            this.sceneView = new ARSCNView();
            this.View.AddSubview(this.sceneView);
        }

        public override void ViewDidLoad()
        {
            base.ViewDidLoad();
            this.sceneView.Frame = this.View.Frame;
        }

        public override void ViewDidAppear(bool animated)
        {
            base.ViewDidAppear(animated);

            this.sceneView.Session.Run(new ARWorldTrackingConfiguration
            {
                LightEstimationEnabled = true,
                WorldAlignment = ARWorldAlignment.Gravity,
            });

            var planeNode = new PlaneNode(width: 0.3f, length: 0.3f,
            UIColor.LightGray);
            this.sceneView.Scene.RootNode.AddChildNode(planeNode);

            SCNNode boxNode = new SCNNode();

            var boxMaterial = new SCNMaterial();
            boxMaterial.Diffuse.Contents = UIColor.Blue;

            var boxGeometry = SCNBox.Create(0.04f, 0.06f, 0.04f, 0f);
            boxNode.Geometry = boxGeometry;
```

```
        boxNode.Geometry.FirstMaterial = boxMaterial;
        boxNode.PhysicsBody = SCNPhysicsBody.CreateDynamicBody();
        boxNode.Position = new SCNVector3(0.0f, 0.05f, 0.0f);

        this.sceneView.Scene.RootNode.AddChildNode(boxNode);
    }

    public override void TouchesEnded(NSSet touches, UIEvent evt)
    {
        base.TouchesEnded(touches, evt);

        if (!(touches.AnyObject is UITouch touch))
            return;

        var point = touch.LocationInView(this.sceneView);
        var hits = this.sceneView.HitTest(point, new
        SCNHitTestOptions());
        var hit = hits.FirstOrDefault();

        if (hit == null)
            return;

        var node = hit.Node;

        if (node == null)
            return;

        var forcePower = 10;
        var pointOfView = this.sceneView.PointOfView;
        var transform = pointOfView.Transform;
        var orientation = new SCNVector3(-transform.M31, -transform.
        M32, -transform.M33);

        node.PhysicsBody.ApplyForce(
            new SCNVector3(
                orientation.X * forcePower,
                orientation.Y * forcePower,
                orientation.Z * forcePower), true);
    }
```

```csharp
    public override void ViewDidDisappear(bool animated)
    {
        base.ViewDidDisappear(animated);
        this.sceneView.Session.Pause();
    }

    public override void DidReceiveMemoryWarning()
    {
        base.DidReceiveMemoryWarning();
    }
}

public class PlaneNode : SCNNode
{
    public PlaneNode(float width, float length, UIColor color)
    {
        Geometry = CreateGeometry(width, length, color);
        PhysicsBody = SCNPhysicsBody.CreateKinematicBody();
        EulerAngles = new SCNVector3((float)(-Math.PI / 2), 0, 0);
    }

    private static SCNGeometry CreateGeometry(float width, float
    length, UIColor color)
    {
        var material = new SCNMaterial();
        material.Diffuse.Contents = color;
        material.DoubleSided = true;

        var geometry = SCNPlane.Create(width, length);
        geometry.Materials = new[] { material };
        return geometry;
    }
}
```

```
public class CubeNode : SCNNode
{
    public CubeNode(float size, UIColor color)
    {
        Geometry = CreateGeometry(size, color);
        Position = new SCNVector3(0, size / 2, 0);
        PhysicsBody = SCNPhysicsBody.CreateDynamicBody();
    }

    private static SCNGeometry CreateGeometry(float size, UIColor
    color)
    {
        var material = new SCNMaterial();
        material.Diffuse.Contents = color;

        var geometry = SCNBox.Create(size, size, size, 0);
        geometry.Materials = new[] { material };
        return geometry;
    }
}
```

There are quite a lot of physics-related variables you can change in SceneKit including Mass and Friction. By altering these values, you will alter how the items in your scene are effected by physics.

---

**Note**   In the same way we can apply force to an object, we are able to apply torque to an object, that is, spinning an object on its axis. You can do this by calling SCNPhysicsBody.ApplyTorque().

---

# Things to Try

Here are a number of different things you could try when experimenting and learning about physics in ARKit.

**Try altering Friction and Mass and other physics properties.**
Play around with altering some of the properties of objects in the scene including their Friction and Mass and see how this effects how they behave in the scene.

**Use ApplyForce() to fire objects.**

Play around with firing objects in different directions and at other objects. See if you can knock other objects over.

**Use different shaped objects.**

Don't just use cubes, for example, see how a sphere may roll down an inclined plane.

**Use ApplyTorque() to apply torque to objects.**

See how different shaped objects with different physics properties behave when you apply torque to them.

# Summary

SceneKit gives us quite a complex physics engine at our disposal. Having items in your scene respond to interactions just like real objects can add yet another level of realism to your AR experiences. You can see how some games make good use of the built-in physics engine in ARKit.

In previous chapters, we have seen how we can use ARKit for image detection, face detection, and plane detection. In the next chapter, we will look at how we can identify 3D items in a scene. Sound impossible? Well, let's find out using Object Detection.

# CHAPTER 15

# Object Detection

Previously, in Chapter 10, "Image Detection," we looked at how we can get our AR mobile app to recognize and respond to predefined 2D images when they are detected in our scenes. Well, in a similar way, we can get our app to respond to predefined 3D objects. It's a more complex process than 2D image recognition; however, ARKit makes this possible. All we need to do is plumb the functionality together.

This process requires two parts, the first to enable the user to use the app to scan a 3D object and store some of its "spatial data," then a second part to use that spatial data again to detect the object in the scene.

While this chapter gives an overview of the concept, the code required to demonstrate this is too long to include in full. Fortunately, Microsoft have created an open source Xamarin Body Detection sample app that we can download and try out.

The example app and resulting screenshots discussed and shown in this chapter are from the Microsoft Xamarin.iOS Scanning App sample here:

https://docs.microsoft.com/en-us/samples/xamarin/ios-samples/ios12-scanninganddetecting3dobjects/

## Scanning and Saving Object Spatial Data

During scanning, an instance of ARObjectScanningConfiguration configuration is used by the Session as can be seen in Listing 15-1.

*Listing 15-1.* Using ARObjectScanningConfiguration

```
var configuration = new ARObjectScanningConfiguration();
sceneView.Session.Run(configuration);
```

When the example app is ran, you will see that during the scanning stage a bounding box is used to denote the area in which the 3D object we wish to scan should be located as seen in Figure 15-1. By default, it detects a horizontal plane and places the bottom of the bounding box on top of it. It is possible to increase the size and location of the bounding box using pinch and pan touch gestures.

***Figure 15-1.*** *Position the bounding box around the object you wish to scan*

Once you are happy that your 3D object is located within the bounding box, press the Scan button to store the spatial data for later use. During the scan, the app asks you to move around the object to allow scanning and subsequent recognition from different angles. This process of scanning from different angles makes the bounding box walls go solid as shown in Figure 15-2. When you are happy that you have scanned the object from a sufficient number of different angles, press Finish.

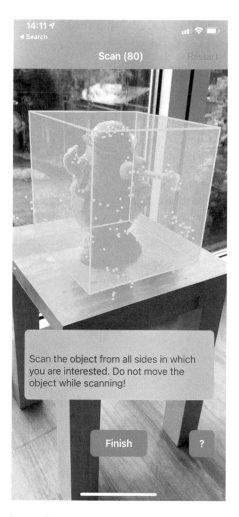

*Figure 15-2.* *Scan the object from multiple directions*

Once the scan is complete, the scanned object is stored as an `ARReferenceObject` in the app for later reference.

# Recognizing Scanned Objects

In order to recognize the 3D object in the scene, we need to retrieve (or at least reference) the previously scanned and saved spatial data for the 3D object and use it to allow the app to detect any objects that match it.

When you are ready, press the "Test" button in the app which will begin detection of the 3D object you have scanned in the scene.

If the object is detected in the scene (using the code in Listing 15-2), the app notifies you and tells you how long it took to detect it (pretty quick in my opinion) as shown in Figure 15-3.

***Listing 15-2.*** The code that fires when the object is detected

```
public override void DidAddNode(ISCNSceneRenderer renderer, SCNNode node,
ARAnchor anchor)
{
    if (anchor != null && anchor is ARObjectAnchor)
    {
        var objectAnchor = anchor as ARObjectAnchor;
        if (objectAnchor.ReferenceObject == referenceObject)
        {
            // Successful detection, do something
        }
    }
}
```

We could do anything once we have successfully detected the object, we could show a message as shown in Figure 15-3, or we could add additional nodes to or next to the detected object.

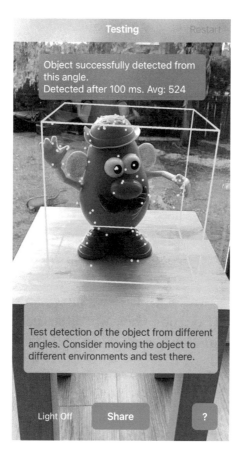

*Figure 15-3.* *Successfully detecting object*

# Things to Try

Here are some ideas of things to try using Object Detection.

**Scan and store multiple objects.**

See if you can scan and store multiple different objects.

**Scan a product and retrieve/display product information upon successful detection.**

Scan and save the 3D characteristics of a product (such as a cuddly toy); then when it is detected, display additional information next to it such as product details, description, price, and so on.

**Scan someone's head to see how accurate recognition is.**

Try scanning someone's head and seeing if Object Detection can recognize it.

**See how small/big an object you can scan and detect.**

Play around with scanning very small or very large objects to see if there are limitations to how well object detection works with very small or very large objects.

**Change the color of the bounding box.**

Try changing the color or other aspects of the bounding box used for scanning and detection.

# Summary

The built-in Object Detection functionality in ARKit continues to show just how varied and powerful ARKit is and literally adds another dimension to the 2D image detection we previously looked at opening up a whole bunch of interesting use cases.

Continuing the theme of detecting interesting subjects in our scene, in the next chapter, we will look at Body Detection where we will see how ARKit can determine the position and orientation of a person in a scene.

# CHAPTER 16

# Body Tracking

When it comes to people, as well as detecting and tracking faces as we saw in Chapter 11, "Face Tracking and Expression Detection," we can also use ARKit to detect bodies in a scene including the orientation of different parts of the body in real time. This is called body tracking, and it gives us the ability to not track the position of major body joints to a high degree of accuracy.

## Detecting a Body in a Scene

We will look at how ARKit is able to detect the presence of a human body in a scene and its various joints and then overlay them on top of the detected body in 3D space. But what exactly are we tracking you ask?

The position of the following joints is tracked:

- Root (center of the hip)
- Head
- LeftHand
- RightHand
- LeftFoot
- RightFoot
- LeftShoulder
- RightShoulder

These values are from the enum ARSkeletonJointName.

© Lee Englestone 2021
L. Englestone, *.NET Developer's Guide to Augmented Reality in iOS*,
https://doi.org/10.1007/978-1-4842-6770-7_16

A number of other joints can be referenced in a detected ARSkeleton3D object (92 in total shown in Figure 16-1). However, only the preceding joints are tracked, so the others are inferred based on the position of these tracked joints.

In fact, in order to get a full list of all 92 joint names that we will iterate over, we will use the string[] returned from calling ARSkeletonDefinition. DefaultBody3DSkeletonDefinition.JointNames.

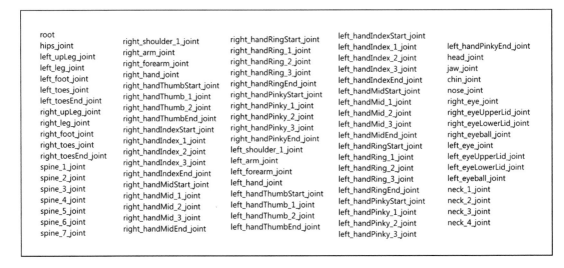

***Figure 16-1.*** *The names of all 92 joints that make up an ARSkeleton*

To enable body tracking in our scene, we use an ARBodyTrackingConfiguration when we run our ARSession as can be seen in Listing 16-1.

---

**Note**    As well as these joints, if we wanted, we could extrapolate the paths between those joints and draw straight lines, thereby creating a visualization of a skeleton.

---

***Listing 16-1.*** Using ARBodyTrackingConfiguration and declaring the SceneViewDelegate

```
public BodyDetectionViewController()
{
    this.sceneView = new ARSCNView
    {
```

```
        AutoenablesDefaultLighting = true,
        Delegate = new SceneViewDelegate()
    };

    this.View.AddSubview(this.sceneView);
}

...


public override void ViewDidAppear(bool animated)
{
    base.ViewDidAppear(animated);

    var bodyTrackingConfiguration
        = new ARBodyTrackingConfiguration()
    {
        WorldAlignment = ARWorldAlignment.Gravity
    };

    this.sceneView.Session.Run(bodyTrackingConfiguration);
}
```

When a body is detected in the scene, an ARBodyAnchor is placed at the relevant location. We can add our custom code to the DidAddNode and DidUpdateNode methods on the ARSCNViewDelegate as shown in Listing 16-2.

As you can also see in Listing 16-2, we have declared a JointNode class that just inherits from SCNNode to represent the joint nodes we want to place in the scene. We are storing these joint nodes in a Dictionary using the joint name as a key when we detect them in DidAddNode. We then update their position by calling .Update(SCNVector3 position) if we detect their position has changed when DidUpdateNode is fired.

We have a method for creating a sphere to represent the joint called MakeJoint(string jointName) which is pretty simple and similar to previous examples we've seen that create basic colored shapes.

The more complex method GetJointPosition(ARBodyAnchor bodyAnchor, string jointName) is taking the detected ARBodyAnchor and calculating and then returning the position of the joint referred to by jointName. It does this by determining the requested joints offset from the root position of the bodyAnchor (which is always the center of the hip). We are also making use of an extension method that converts an NMatrix4 to a SCNMatrix4.

The end result shows 92 spheres in the scene arranged in the same orientation as the detected body. The orientation and position of these spheres change as the orientation and position of the tracked body change in real time.

*Listing 16-2.* Detecting and updating body joint positions

```
public class SceneViewDelegate : ARSCNViewDelegate
{
    Dictionary<string, JointNode> joints
        = new Dictionary<string, JointNode>();

      public override void DidAddNode(
         ISCNSceneRenderer renderer, SCNNode node,
         ARAnchor anchor)
      {
          if (!(anchor is ARBodyAnchor bodyAnchor))
              return;

          foreach (var jointName in ARSkeletonDefinition.
          DefaultBody3DSkeletonDefinition.JointNames)
          {
              JointNode jointNode = MakeJoint(jointName);

              var jointPosition = GetJointPosition(bodyAnchor,
              jointName);
              jointNode.Position = jointPosition;

              if (!joints.ContainsKey(jointName))
              {
                  node.AddChildNode(jointNode);
                  joints.Add(jointName, jointNode);
              }
          }
      }

      public override void DidUpdateNode(
         ISCNSceneRenderer renderer, SCNNode node,
           ARAnchor anchor)
      {
```

```
    if (!(anchor is ARBodyAnchor bodyAnchor))
        return;

    foreach (var jointName in ARSkeletonDefinition.
    DefaultBody3DSkeletonDefinition.JointNames)
    {
        var jointPosition = GetJointPosition(bodyAnchor,
        jointName);

        if (joints.ContainsKey(jointName))
        {
            joints[jointName].Update(jointPosition);
        }
    }
}

private SCNVector3 GetJointPosition(
    ARBodyAnchor bodyAnchor, string jointName)
{
    NMatrix4 jointTransform = bodyAnchor.Skeleton.
    GetModelTransform((NSString)jointName);
    return new SCNVector3(jointTransform.Column3);
}

private JointNode MakeJoint(string jointName)
{
    var jointNode = new JointNode();

    var material = new SCNMaterial();
    material.Diffuse.Contents =
        GetJointColour(jointName);

    var jointGeometry =
        SCNSphere.Create(GetJointRadius(jointName));
    jointGeometry.FirstMaterial = material;
    jointNode.Geometry = jointGeometry;

    return jointNode;
}
```

```
private UIColor GetJointColour(string jointName)
{
    switch (jointName)
    {
        case "root":
        case "left_foot_joint":
        case "right_foot_joint":
        case "left_leg_joint":
        case "right_leg_joint":
        case "left_hand_joint":
        case "right_hand_joint":
        case "left_arm_joint":
        case "right_arm_joint":
        case "left_forearm_joint":
        case "right_forearm_joint":
        case "head_joint":
            return UIColor.Green;
    }

    return UIColor.White;
}

private float GetJointRadius(string jointName)
{
    switch (jointName)
    {
        case "root":
        case "left_foot_joint":
        case "right_foot_joint":
        case "left_leg_joint":
        case "right_leg_joint":
        case "left_hand_joint":
        case "right_hand_joint":
        case "left_arm_joint":
        case "right_arm_joint":
        case "left_forearm_joint":
```

```
                case "right_forearm_joint":
                case "head_joint":
                    return 0.04f;
            }

            if (jointName.Contains("hand"))
                return 0.01f;

            return 0.02f;
        }
    }

public class JointNode : SCNNode
    {
        public void Update(SCNVector3 position)
        {
            this.Position = position;
        }
    }
}
```

The result can be seen in Figure 16-2. The tracked bodies' major joints are tracked and shown as green spheres and other inferred minor joints shown as white nodes.

As usual, the accuracy of ARKit's ability to track things in the real world depends on sufficient lighting. To give ARKit the best chance of tracking a body in a scene, make sure the environment is well lit.

*Figure 16-2. Showing the orientation of the tracked body using nodes*

# Capturing Body Motion

One use of body tracking is to translate the detected movements and positions of the tracked body and mimic them on a humanoid shaped 3D model (called a rig) so that if you move your arm, the 3D model's arm also moves in the same manner. This requires creating a 3D model with various moving joints and importing it into the app, something that is beyond the scope of this book but can be seen in Figure 16-3.

To learn more about model rigging with body tracking, see Apple's documentation (`https://developer.apple.com/documentation/arkit/rigging_a_model_for_ motion_capture`).

***Figure 16-3.***  *Rigging of body tracking example*

# Potential Applications

Because we can detect the position of the major joints and their relative position to one another, we can infer the angles of various parts of the body in the scene. I have seen this technology used to automatically detect if a user is slouching when sitting at their desk to help prevent unnecessary pressure on the spine and to help avoid backache.

Being able to detect repetitive body movements makes Body Detection a great way to track exercises such as press-ups and squats.

# Things to Try

Here are a few things you could try yourself when implementing body tracking.

**Change the color, size, and opacity of the nodes representing the joints.**
Play around with representing the joint nodes in different ways.

**Add touch gestures to help identify joints when pressed.**
Use your knowledge of touch gestures so that when you touch a node, it displays the name of it on the screen.

**Try rigging a 3D model to copy your movements.**
Look up how to use an appropriate 3D skeleton model and rig it to the tracked body to have it mimic the movements of the body in the scene.

**Add additional nodes to the tracked body.**
Either use a combination of out of the box geometry shapes, images, or 3D models to add additional nodes to the tracked body. For example, you could place a spherical emoji head at the position of the head node.

**Add straight lines between joints to create a skeleton effect.**
As you know the positions and names of the major and minor joints, you could try and create lines (or long thin boxes/cylinders) between them.

# Summary

If you have got this far, then you probably by now know how to make use of a lot of ARKit's Augmented Reality capabilities and be able to make some rather remarkable AR experiences.

Once you have made your killer AR app, you may wish to share it with the world via the App Store, so in the next and final chapter, we will look at "Publishing to the App Store."

# CHAPTER 17

# Publishing to the App Store

As promised from the very start, everything we have looked at in this book has been possible to experiment with and put into your app and deploy onto your phone without an Apple Developer Account.

That said, if what you have created is ready to be shared with the rest of the world, you are going to want to put it in the App Store for others to download and install. To do this, you will need an Apple Developer Account, and you will need to follow the steps outlined in this chapter.

## App Store Submission To-Do List

In this chapter, we will cover the process of getting your app into the App Store. The process is comprised of a number of stages:

- Set up icons for the app.

- Set up the launch screen (optional).

- Set up App ID and Entitlements.

- Create and install an App Store provisioning profile.

- Update the build release configuration.

- Build your app and submit it to Apple.

© Lee Englestone 2021
L. Englestone, *.NET Developer's Guide to Augmented Reality in iOS*,
https://doi.org/10.1007/978-1-4842-6770-7_17

# Set Up Icons for the App

Because the icon for your app will be used in a variety of different places, you will need to provide the icon in several different sizes.

Your icon will appear in different sizes in the following places:

- App Store

- Notifications

- Settings

- Spotlight

To provide different sized icons, open `Assets.xcassets` and provide images for an IconImage resource. See in Figure 17-1.

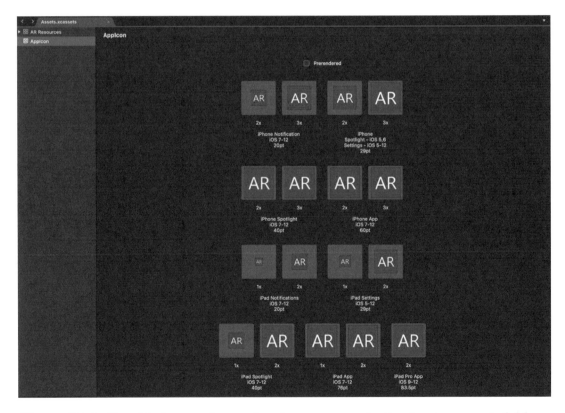

*Figure 17-1.* *Provide images for an AppIcon resource in the Assets.xcassets folder*

# Set Up Launch Screen Image

The launch screen for your app is the screen that you see immediately after launching your app but before you initially see the main page of your app and by default it is a blank white screen. And fortunately, it is very easy to change if you choose to do so. It is something I recommend because it is relatively simple and can help with the initial experience a user has with your app.

As mentioned, you optionally can override the default blank launch screen of your app (LaunchScreen.storyboard). Once you open LaunchScreen.storyboard, you can change its background color and add labels and images to it as can be seen in Figure 17-2. If you go ahead and choose to alter the default, when your app launches, the updated launch screen will be shown before your main app.

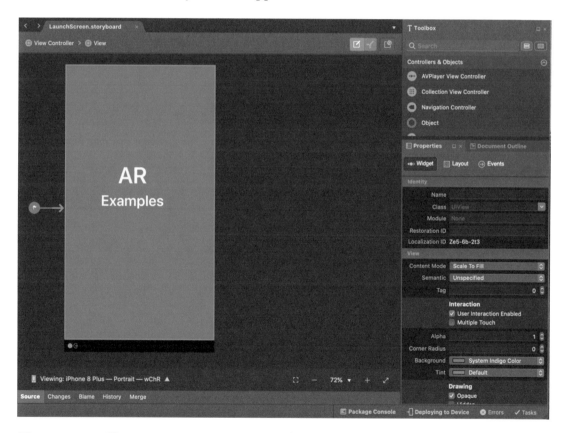

***Figure 17-2.*** *You can customize your app's launch screen*

# Set Up App ID and Entitlements

Before you go much further, you will need to create an App ID for your app. You do this in the Apple Developer Portal at `https://developer.apple.com`, and to be able to do this, you will need an Apple Developer Account which at the time of writing costs £79.

Also, if you do not already have an Apple ID, you will need to create one first at `https://appleid.apple.com/account`.

When you log in to your Apple Developer Account, you should be greeted by a page as shown in Figure 17-3.

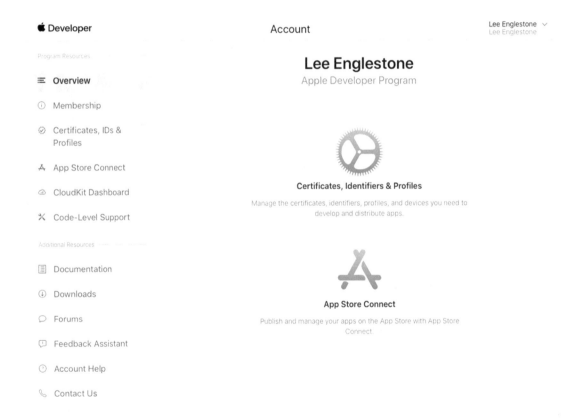

***Figure 17-3.*** *Your Apple Developer Account*

Okay, presuming you've got your Apple Developer Account now and have logged in, go to Certificates, IDs & Profiles as shown in Figure 17-4.

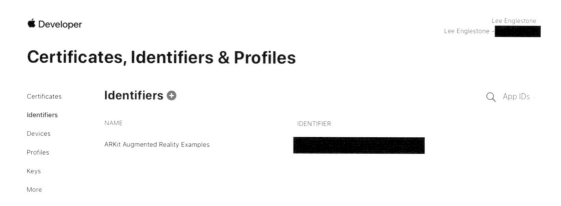

**Figure 17-4.** *The identifiers section of your developer account*

We are going to create a new Identifier for our app in the form of an App ID, so click the + button next to the Identifiers heading to start creating a new identifier for our app.

Select App IDs from the list of identifiers as shown in Figure 17-5, then press Continue.

 Developer

Lee Englestone
Lee Englestone –

# Certificates, Identifiers & Profiles

‹ All Identifiers

## Register a new identifier

Continue

○ **App IDs**
Register an App ID to enable your app, app extensions, or App Clip to access available services and identify your app in a provisioning profile. You can enable app services when you create an App ID or modify these settings later.

**Services IDs**
For each website that uses Sign in with Apple, register a services identifier (Services ID), configure your domain and return URL, and create an associated private key.

**Pass Type IDs**
Register a pass type identifier (Pass Type ID) for each kind of pass you create (i.e. gift cards). Registering your Pass Type IDs lets you generate Apple-issued certificates which are used to digitally sign and send updates to your passes, and allow your passes to be recognized by Wallet.

**Website Push IDs**
Register a Website Push Identifier (Website Push ID). Registering your Website Push IDs lets you generate Apple-issued certificates which are used to digitally sign and send push notifications from your website to macOS.

**iCloud Containers**
Registering your iCloud Container lets you use the iCloud Storage APIs to enable your apps to store data and documents in iCloud, keeping your apps up to date automatically.

**App Groups**
Registering your App Group allows access to group containers that are shared among multiple related apps, and allows certain additional interprocess communication between the apps.

**Figure 17-5.** *Beginning to register a new identifier*

On the next screen, select what the App ID is for – in our case, an App, so choose App from the options as shown in Figure 17-6, then press Continue.

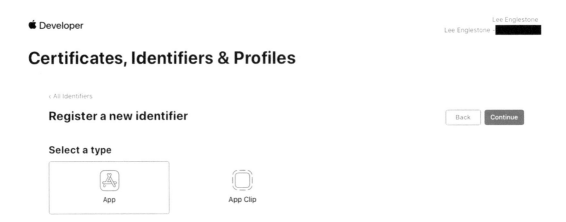

**Figure 17-6.** *Choosing what we are using the App ID for*

In the next screen, provide a *Description* and *Bundle ID*, then select from the list any device Capabilities your app uses as shown in Figure 17-7, then press Continue.

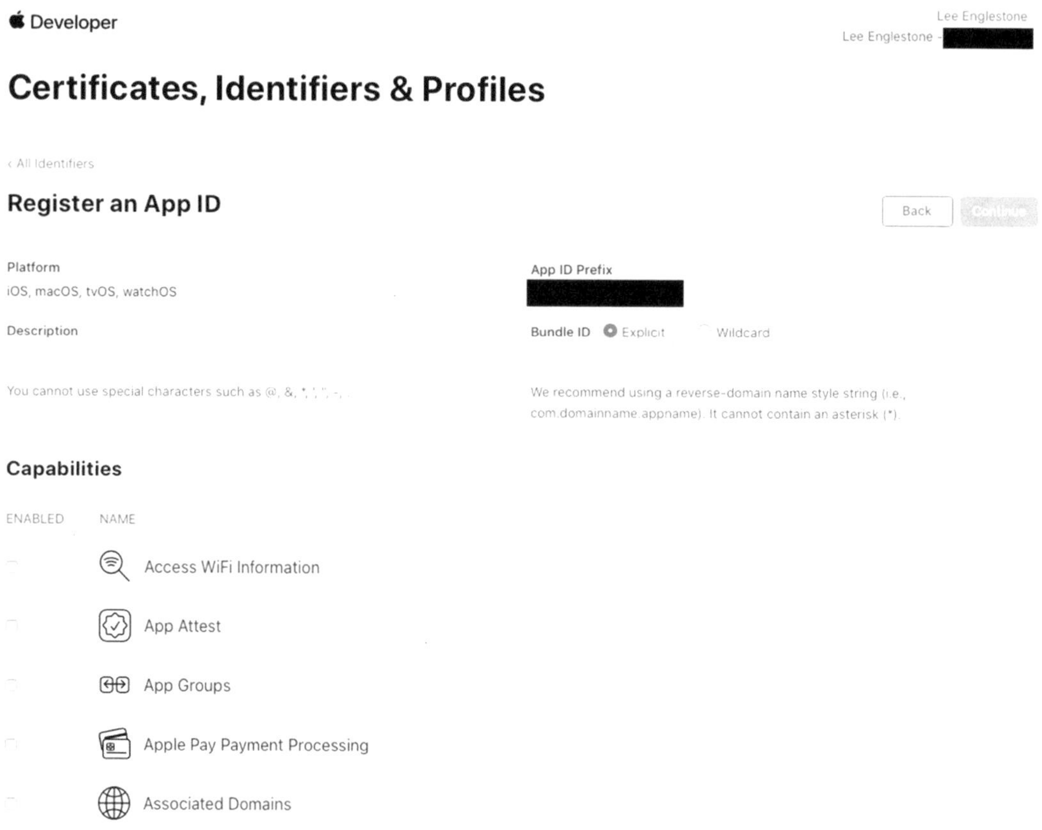

 Developer

Lee Englestone
Lee Englestone - ███████████

# Certificates, Identifiers & Profiles

‹ All Identifiers

## Register an App ID

Back    Continue

| | |
|---|---|
| **Platform** | **App ID Prefix** |
| iOS, macOS, tvOS, watchOS | ████████████ |

| | |
|---|---|
| **Description** | **Bundle ID**  ⦿ Explicit      ○ Wildcard |

You cannot use special characters such as @, &, *, ', ", -, .

We recommend using a reverse-domain name style string (i.e., com.domainname.appname). It cannot contain an asterisk (*).

## Capabilities

| ENABLED | NAME |
|---|---|
| ☐ | 🔍 Access WiFi Information |
| ☐ | ✓ App Attest |
| ☐ | ⊕⊕ App Groups |
| ☐ | 💳 Apple Pay Payment Processing |
| ☐ | 🌐 Associated Domains |

***Figure 17-7.*** *Providing information for your App ID*

On the next screen, you are given a chance to confirm the App ID details before registering as can be seen in Figure 17-8. When ready, press Continue, then press Register.

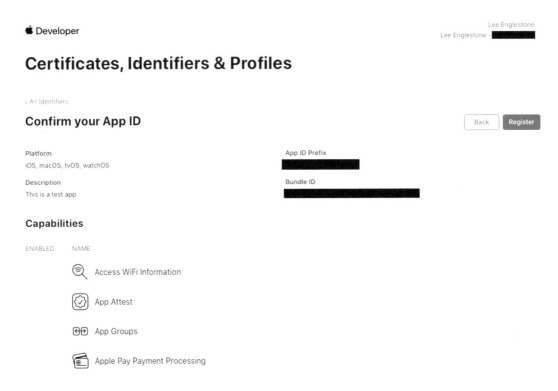

*Figure 17-8.* *Confirm your App ID details before registering*

Congratulations! You have created your first App! Well, App ID anyway. Don't worry. We'll put it to good use soon enough.

# Create and Install an App Store Provisioning Profile

In order to publish your app to the App Store, you will need to create, install, and use an appropriate distribution provisioning profile on your computer. These provisioning profiles contain information about the certificate that is used to sign your app, the App ID, and where it can be installed.

To create and install a provisioning profile for your app, go to *Certificates, IDs & Profiles* section in the Apple Developer Portal again.

This time, go to the *Profiles* section. From here, you will see any existing Development or Distribution profiles and can create new ones.

In the Profiles section, click the + button next to the Profiles heading as shown in Figure 17-9.

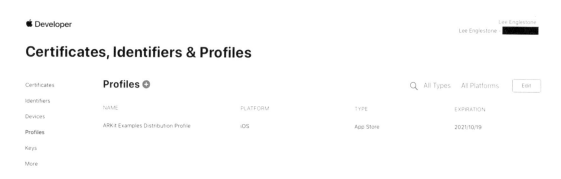

*Figure 17-9.* *Development and Distribution profiles*

Then on the *Register a New Provisioning Profile* page, under the *Distribution* section, select App Store as shown in Figure 17-10 and press Continue.

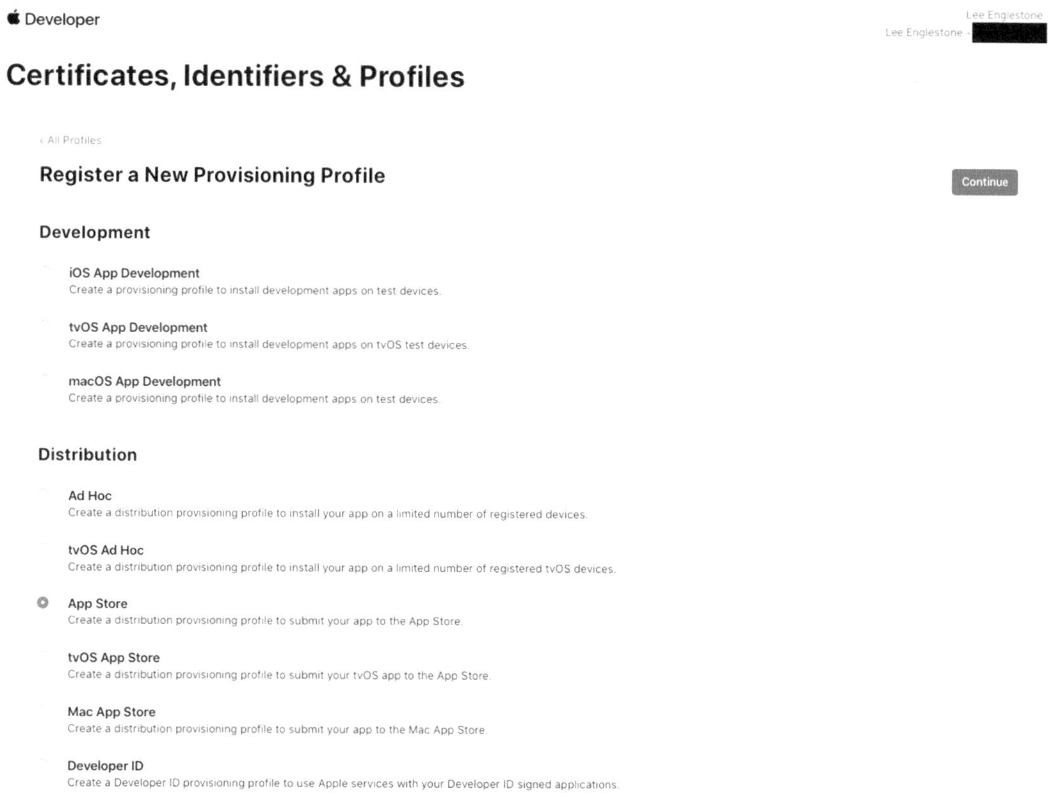

 Developer

**Certificates, Identifiers & Profiles**

‹ All Profiles

**Register a New Provisioning Profile**                                   Continue

**Development**

iOS App Development
Create a provisioning profile to install development apps on test devices.

tvOS App Development
Create a provisioning profile to install development apps on tvOS test devices.

macOS App Development
Create a provisioning profile to install development apps on test devices.

**Distribution**

Ad Hoc
Create a distribution provisioning profile to install your app on a limited number of registered devices.

tvOS Ad Hoc
Create a distribution provisioning profile to install your app on a limited number of registered tvOS devices.

App Store
Create a distribution provisioning profile to submit your app to the App Store.

tvOS App Store
Create a distribution provisioning profile to submit your tvOS app to the App Store.

Mac App Store
Create a distribution provisioning profile to submit your app to the Mac App Store.

Developer ID
Create a Developer ID provisioning profile to use Apple services with your Developer ID signed applications.

*Figure 17-10.* *Registering a new distribution provisioning profile*

On the next screen, select your App ID from the drop-down list as shown in Figure 17-11 and press Continue.

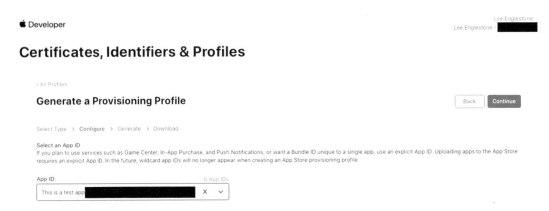

***Figure 17-11.***  *Select the App the provisioning profile is for*

Select the certificate from the next screen as shown in Figure 17-12, then press Continue.

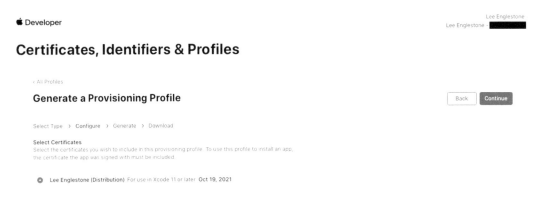

***Figure 17-12.***  *Select certificate*

Provide a name for the Provisioning Profile on the next screen as shown in Figure 17-13, then press Generate.

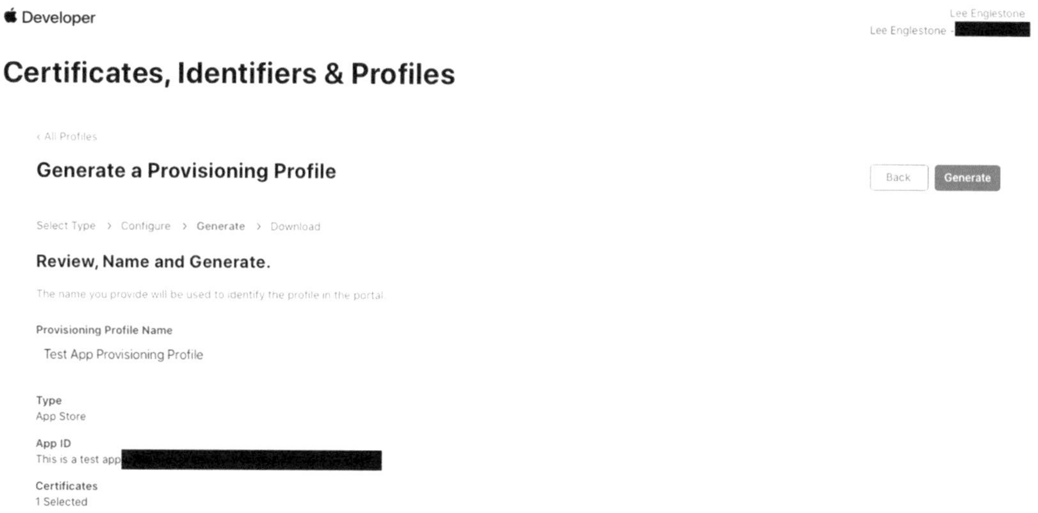

**Figure 17-13.** *Provide a name for the provisioning profile*

Then finally, as shown in Figure 17-14, download and double-click the Provisioning Profile you have generated to install it to your computer.

**Figure 17-14.** *Download and install the provisioning profile*

Phew, now you will have successfully installed a distribution provisioning profile onto your machine that can be used to put your app in the App Store.

Now, let's go and build the version of the app we wish to upload in the next section.

# Update Build Release Configuration

Before we build our app for submission to the App Store, we need to do a few more things including assigning the Provisioning Profile we created in the previous section.

Open the Info.plist file and go to the Application tab. It will probably look a bit like this. Make sure *Manual Provisioning* is selected as the *Signing Scheme* as shown in Figure 17-15.

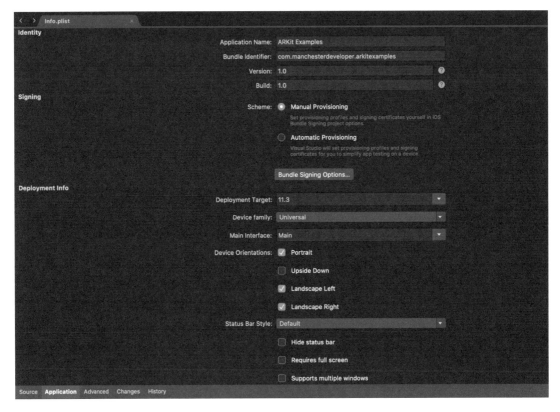

***Figure 17-15.*** *Ensure Signing is using Manual Provisioning*

Next, open your *Project Options* and go to *Build* ➤ *IOS Build*. On this page, change the *Configuration* to *Release* and *Platform* to *Phone*, and ensure all other settings look like the following in Figure 17-16.

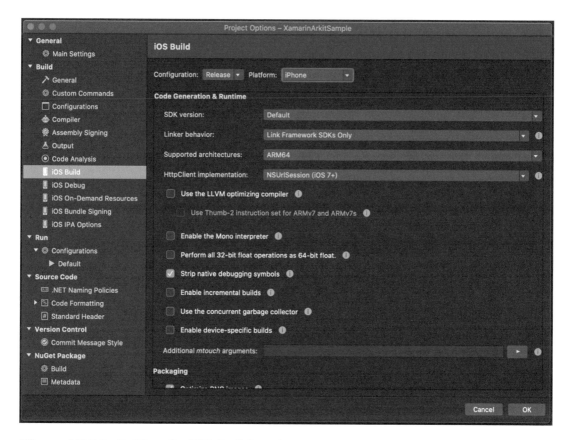

**Figure 17-16.** *Setting the iOS Build settings*

Next, go to the *iOS Bundle Signing* section as shown in Figure 17-17.

- The *Configuration* should be set to *Release* and the *Platform* set to *iPhone*.

- The *Signing Identity* should be *Distribution (Automatic)*.

- The *Provisioning Profile* should be the one you created in the previous step.

**Note**    You will only see Provisioning Profiles that have a bundle ID that match the app's bundle ID in the `Info.plist` file.

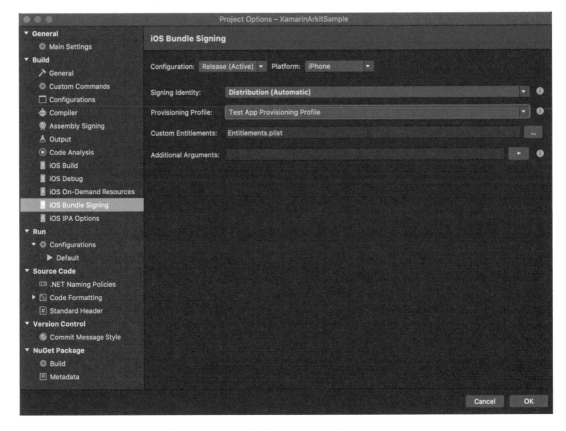

*Figure 17-17.*  *Setting the iOS Bundle Signing settings*

Your project should now be ready to build and publish. But first, we need to get the App Store side of things ready to receive the upload of the app.

# Set Up the App in App Store Connect

Before you can submit your app to the Apple for review, you must first configure it in App Store Connect. App Store Connect is an online portal used to manage your iOS apps in the App Store and can be found at `https://appstoreconnect.apple.com/`.

There are a number of things we need to do in App Store Connect including

- Provide app name as will appear in store

- Select Bundle ID

- Provide description, keywords, category

- Provide screenshots

- Declare price and availability

The main screen of the App Store Connect looks like the following in Figure 17-18.

**Figure 17-18.** *App Store Connect*

Go to *My Apps* and create a new app by pressing the blue circle + button next to the Apps heading and provide your app's details as shown in Figure 17-19.

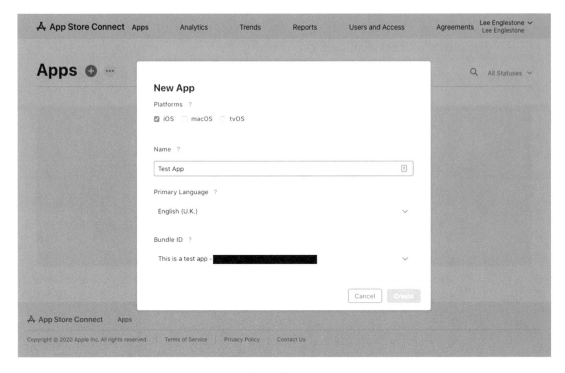

***Figure 17-19.*** *Creating a new app from the Apps section*

Once you have created an app in App Store Connect you should see a screen as shown in Figure 17-20, where you can provide further details for it.

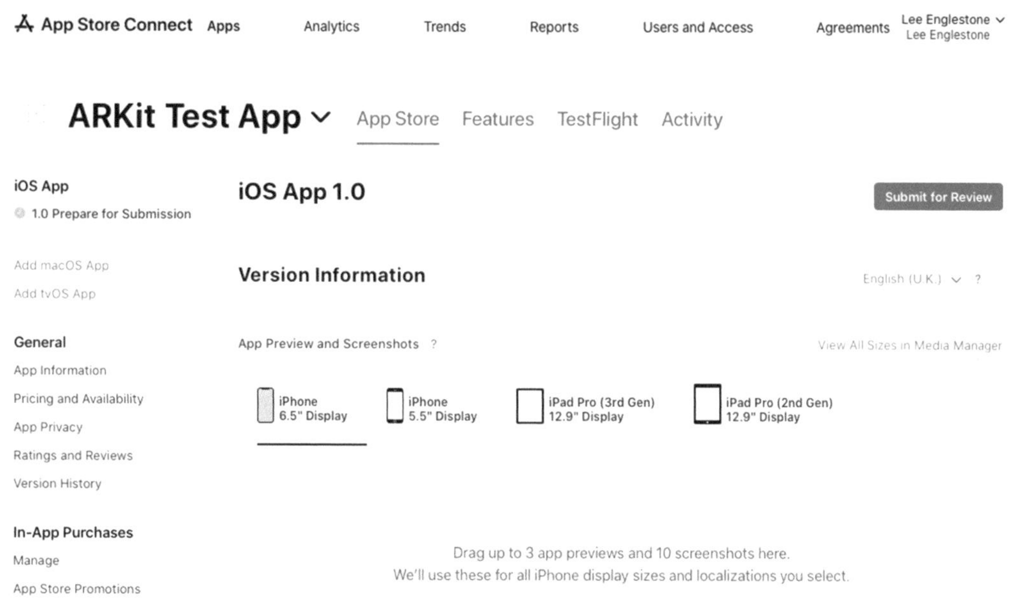

**Figure 17-20.** *Your draft unpublished app*

In the *Pricing and Availability* section shown in Figure 17-21, you can set how much or how little you would like to charge for your app.

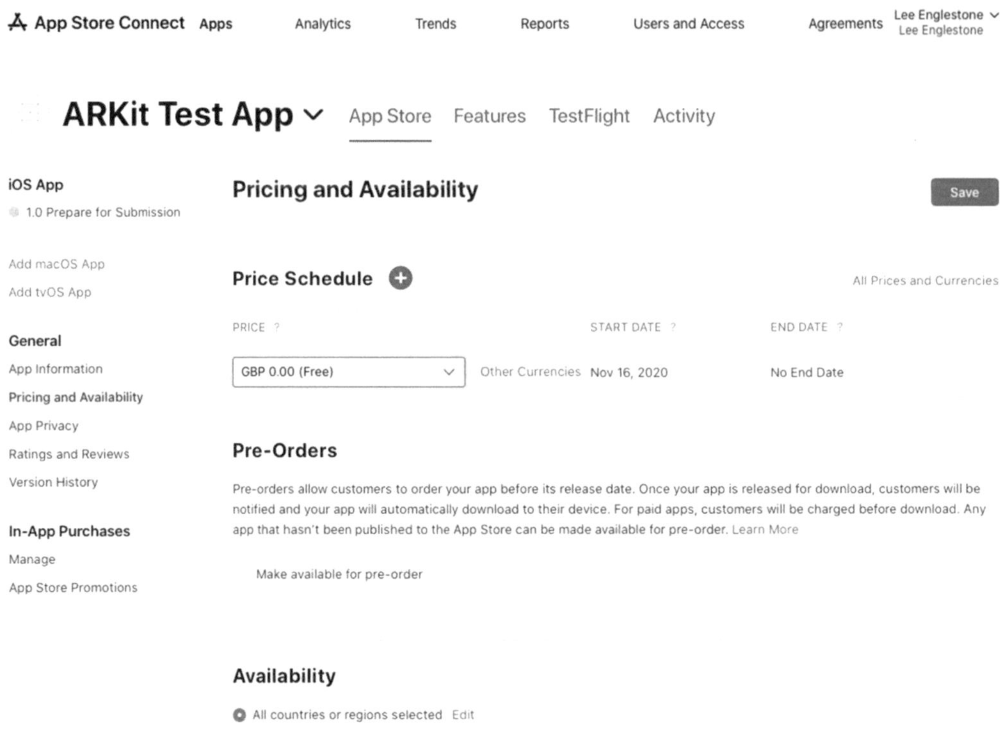

**Figure 17-21.** *Providing pricing information*

In the *General Information* section, you should provide your app's *Primary Category* and *Secondary Category* as well as a *Subtitle* to aid people searching for apps like yours and give them the best chance of stumbling onto your app. See Figure 17-22.

You will also need to set up the *Content Rights* for the app where you confirm that you have rights to any content in the app.

**ARKit Test App** ˅   App Store   Features   TestFlight   Activity

iOS App

☑ 1.0 Prepare for Submission

Add macOS App

Add tvOS App

**General**

App Information

Pricing and Availability

App Privacy

Ratings and Reviews

Version History

**In-App Purchases**

Manage

App Store Promotions

**App Information**

This information is used for all platforms of this app. Any changes will be released with your next app version.

**Localizable Information**                                                          English (U.K.) ˅   ?

Name   ?

ARKit Test App

Subtitle   ?

**General Information**

Bundle ID   ?                                        Primary Language   ?

This is a test app - ███████████████ ˅      English (U.K.)

                                                     Category   ?

SKU   ?

ManchesterDeveloperTestApp1                          Primary                              ˅

Apple ID   ?                                         Secondary (optional)                 ˅

***Figure 17-22.*** *Providing general app information*

But don't press Submit for Review yet as you will need to create and upload/ associate a build with your initial release. For this, we need to go back to Visual Studio for Mac which we will see in the next section.

# Build the App and Submit It to Apple

Now that you have set up your app in App Store Connect, you need to finally build and submit your app.

Select the Release Build Configuration in Visual Studio for Mac as shown in Figure 17-23.

***Figure 17-23.*** *Setting to Release build configuration*

Then, from the *Build* menu, select *Archive for Publishing* as shown in Figure 17-24. This bundles up your app into an archive ready for upload.

***Figure 17-24.*** *Archiving your app for Publishing*

Once the Archive has been created, click the *Sign and Distribute* button shown in Figure 17-25.

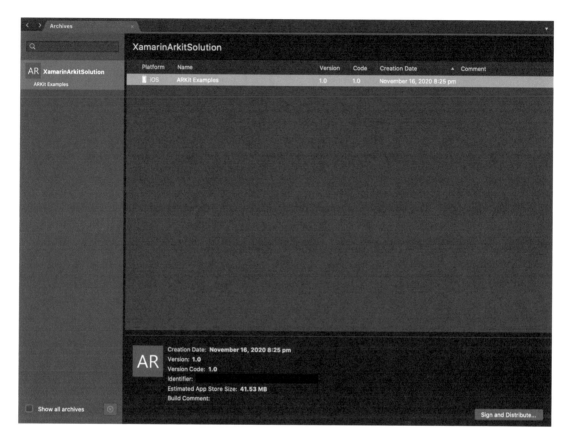

**Figure 17-25.** *After Archive creation*

On the Select iOS Distribution Channel screen, select App Store and press Next as shown in Figure 17-26.

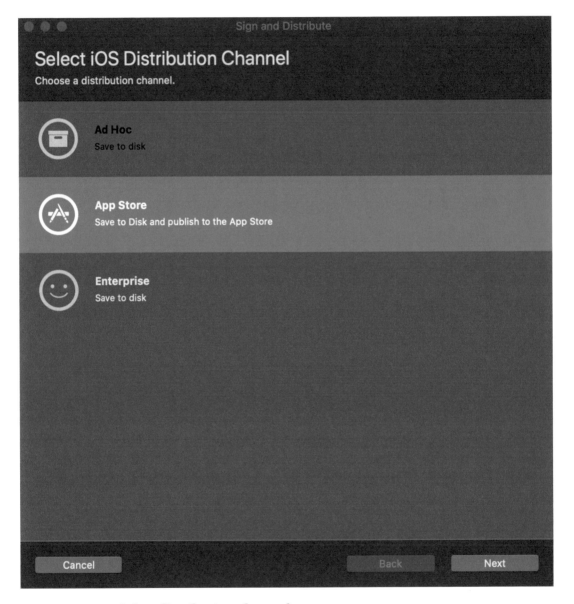

***Figure 17-26.*** *Select distribution channel*

In the next screen, when selecting a destination, choose *Upload*, then Next as shown in Figure 17-27.

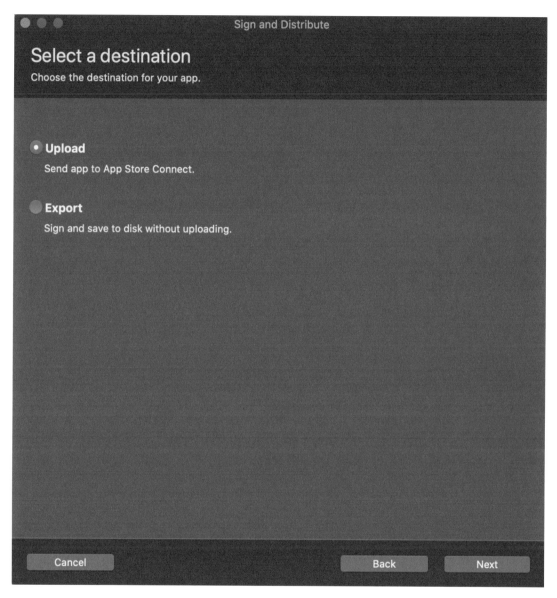

**Figure 17-27.**  *Select destination*

In the next Provisioning Profile screen as shown in Figure 17-28, select the desired provisioning profile (if you have more than one), then press Next.

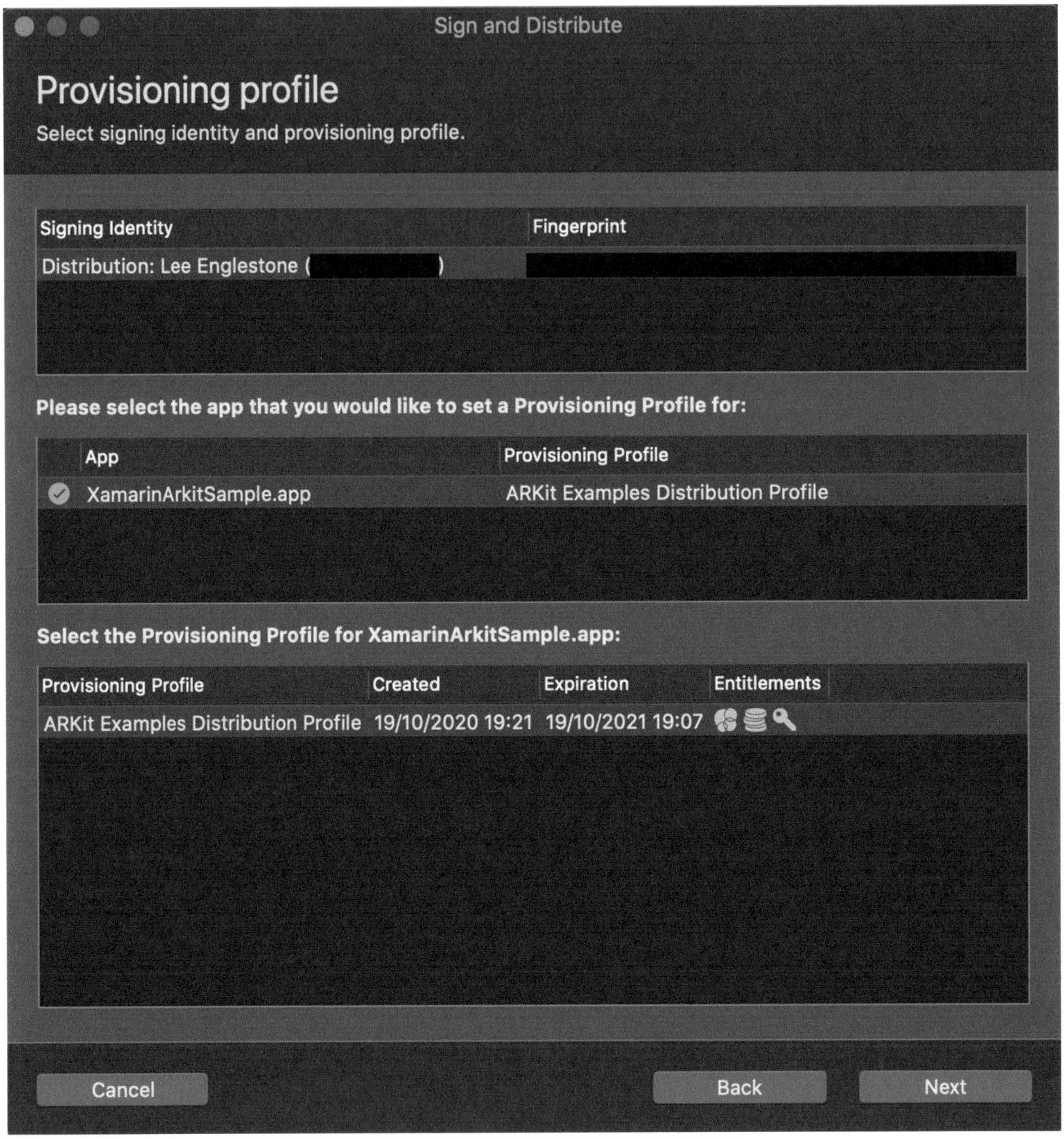

***Figure 17-28.***  *Select the relevant provisioning profile*

On the next screen, you will be asked to provide some credentials to enable communication with App Store Connect as shown in Figure 17-29.

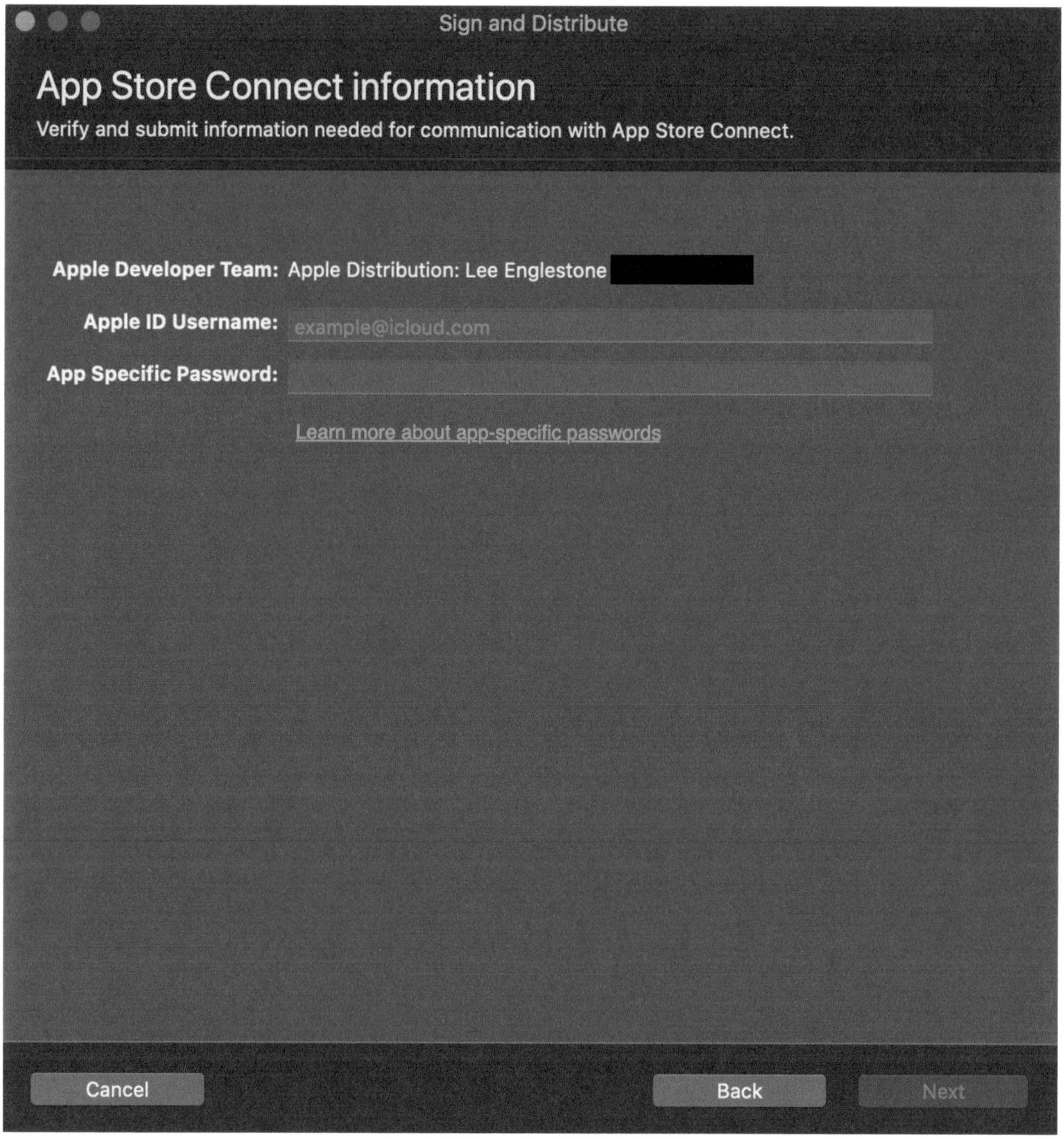

**Figure 17-29.** *Provide communication details for the App Store*

Now you may wonder what on earth this App Specific Password is. I certainly did.

It turns out you must create a dedicated app password at `https://appleid.apple.com` as shown in Figure 17-30.

Security        PASSWORD                              TRUSTED PHONE NUMBERS                    Edit
                Change password...

                TWO-FACTOR AUTHENTICATION             APP-SPECIFIC PASSWORDS
                On                                    Generate password...

***Figure 17-30.*** *Provide communication details for the App Store*

After you have generated an app specific password, enter your Apple ID Username and the password and press Next.

After which, as you can guess by the next screen shown in Figure 17-31, you are *finally* ready to publish the app. Press *Publish*.

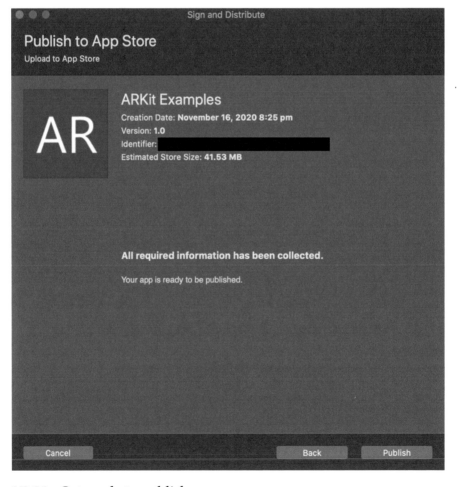

***Figure 17-31.*** *Get ready to publish your app*

Once you have clicked Publish, you will be asked to choose a location to save an ipa file, after which, your app will be uploaded to App Store Connect, and if you have been successful, you will be notified that publishing has succeeded as shown in Figure 17-32.

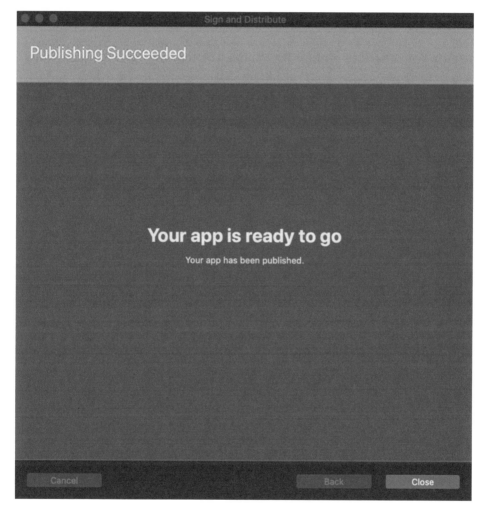

*Figure 17-32.* *Successfully publishing your app to the App Store*

You will notice that the status of your app will change to "Waiting for Review." You just have to wait now for Apple to make its automated and manual checks on your app by its team of reviewers. If Apple have any means to reject your app such as copyright infringement or unclear permission requests, your app will be rejected, and you will be given feedback. If this happens, you will be able to make the relevant changes to your app and resubmit for approval.

Once Apple have successfully approved your app, it will shortly appear in the App Store.

# Summary

Well, that's it. You now have everything you need to not only develop some pretty impressive and useful Augmented Reality experiences but also distribute and share them with the world. What you choose to make next is up to you.

Augmented Reality is set to become increasingly popular over the coming years, and the rich variety of abilities that ARKit allows us to leverage right out of the box to deliver amazing AR experiences should be apparent by now.

The experiences you can create are limited only by your imagination.

Good luck and have fun.

# Index

## A

Anchors, 38
Animations
    combining, 54
    easing, 53
    opacity, 49, 50
    orientation, 51
    position, 51
    repeat behavior, 52
    scale, 50, 51
    wait actions, 54
Apple ID, 1
App Store
    App ID/entitlements
        Certificates/IDs/Profiles, 154, 155
        choose App ID, 156
        description/Bundle ID, 156, 157
        details confirmation, 157, 158
        Developer Account, 154
        new identifier, 155
    Archive for Publishing, 170
    build release configuration
        iOS build settings, 162, 163
        iOS Bundle settings, 163, 164
        signing scheme, 162
    communication details, 174–176
    icons, 152
    iOS distribution channel, 171, 172
    launch screen image, 153

    provisioning profile, 173, 174
        App ID, 160
        development/distribution, 158, 159
        download/install, 161
        naming, 160, 161
        registration, 159
        select certificate, 160
    publishing, 176, 177
    release build configuration, 169
    select destination, 172, 173
    sign/distribute, 170, 171
    stages, 151
App Store Connect, 164
    create new app, 165, 166
    general information, 168, 169
    main screen, 165
    number of things, 164, 165
    pricing information, 167, 168
    provide details, 166, 167
Augmented Reality (AR)
    basic concepts
        camera, 25, 26
        configuration, 28
        Gravity, 25
        GravityAndHeading, 25
        positioning, 21–23
        SceneKit, 21
        SceneView, 19, 20
        Session, 20, 21

© Lee Englestone 2021
L. Englestone, *.NET Developer's Guide to Augmented Reality in iOS*,
https://doi.org/10.1007/978-1-4842-6770-7

Augmented Reality (AR) (*cont.*)
> sizes, 26–28
>> world alignment, 24
>> world origin, 23, 24
> coaching overlay, 45–48
> coordinate axis, 42–44
> feature points, 41, 42
> playing sound, 69
> playing video, 70, 71
> statistics, 44, 45
> world origin, 42–44

## B

Blender, 119, 120
Body tracking
> ARBodyAnchor, 143
> ARBodyTrackingConfiguration, 142, 143
> body motion, 148, 149
> definition, 141
> DidAddNode, 143
> joint names, 142
> joint positions, 144–147
> joints, 141
> orientation, 144, 147, 148
> potential applications, 149, 150

## C

Constraints
> LookAtConstraint, 57, 58
> SCNBillboardConstraint, 57
> types, 58

## D, E

DidUpdateNode method,
> 65, 67, 76, 105, 143

## F

Facial expressions, 99
> ARFaceTrackingConfiguration, 101
> detectable list, 100, 101
> floating value, 101
> recognizing, 101–104
> SCNFillMode.Lines, 100

## G, H

Geometry
> definition, 33
> shapes, 33–35
Gesture recognizers
> dimensions, 108
> long press, 113
> panning, 112
> pinching, 110, 111
> rotating, 111
> SceneView, 108, 109
> swiping, 113
> tapping, 109, 110
> types, 107
GetJointPosition(ARBodyAnchor
> bodyAnchor, string jointName)
> method, 143

## I

Image detection
> adding images
>> AR Resource
>>> Group, 86, 87
>> AR Resource image, 87
>> Assets.xcassets folder, 86
>> dimensions, 88
>> dynamical, 91

detecting images
    ARImageAnchor, 89
    custom PlaneNode, 91
    declaration, 89
    orientation, 90
    Scene View Delegate, 88–90

## J, K

JointNode class, 143

## L

Lighting
    ARSCNView.
        AutoenablesDefaultLighting, 61
    ARSCNView.Automatically
        UpdatesLighting, 61, 62
    SCNNode, 63
    shadows, 63, 64
        add light sources, 65–67
        IARSCNViewDelegate, 67
        plane detection, 64
        SCNLightingModel.ShadowOnly, 65
        ViewDidAppear, 64
    types, 62

## M

MakeJoint(string jointName) method, 143
Materials
    fill mode, 37
    image, 36, 37
    solid color, 35, 36

## N

Nodes, 31, 32

## O

Object detection
    recognize scanned objects, 137, 139
    spatial data
        ARObjectScanningConfiguration, 135
        bounding box, 136
        scanning, 136, 137
Opacity, 32, 33

## P, Q, R

Physics engine
    applying force, 128–132
    gravity
        applying, 124
        combining, 125–128
    rigid structure, 123, 124
    solid objects, 125–128
Plane detection
    abilities, 73
    applications, 82
    ARPlaneAnchor, 73
    ARSCNViewDelegate, 74, 75
    grid image, 80, 81
    horizontal/vertical planes, 80
    turning off, 81
    ViewController class, 76–80

## S

SCNBox.Create()method, 34
SCNSphere.Create()method, 34
Session.Run() method, 20

## T, U

this.sceneView.Scene.RootNode.
    AddChildNode()method, 27

3D models
    animations, 121
    creation, 119, 120
    importing
        file formats, 117
        SCNNode, 118
        Xcode, 118, 119
    shadows, 121
Tracking faces, 95, 96
    ARFaceAnchor, 97
    ARFaceTrackingConfiguration, 96–98
    ARFaceTrackingConfiguration.
        IsSupported, 96
    Scene View Delegate, 96

## V, W

ViewDidAppear method, 27
Visual Studio
    installation, 3, 4
    project creation

app details, 14, 15
camera permissions, 17, 18
deployment device, 16, 17
project details, 15, 16
type, 13, 14

## X, Y, Z

Xcode
    installation, 2, 3
    project creation, 4, 5
        Apple ID, 9, 10
        Bundle Identifier, 13
        deployment target, 10, 11
        details, 6, 7
        location, 7, 8
        Personal code signing, 13
        Swift project, 8, 9
        team selection, 9, 10
        template, 5, 6
        trust developer, 11–13

Printed in the United States
by Baker & Taylor Publisher Services